ENGAGE, EXCEL,
EXCEED

The business playbook for creating phenomenal performance and championship culture

Jackie,

There is a special place in heaven for all you must put up with!

Jk, I love me some C.R. !

Woody

WOODY SHERWOOD

CONTENTS

PREFACE

According to Gallup, only thirty-three percent of U.S. employees are engaged at work. They collect a paycheck and manage to stay employed while costing businesses billions of dollars a year in lost productivity. Executives and managers point the finger at these workers who aren't enthusiastic, don't seem to buy into the vision of the company, and approach their nine-to-five with apathetic disregard. While in some cases, it is an employee issue, a majority of the time the problem is created unintentionally by a management culture that simply does not have the tools to build engagement. This missing link in the evolution of the engagement conundrum can be found in athletics.

In my former life—NCAA D1 college coaching—to stay employed, you needed to do at least one thing at an elite level: *engage your student-athletes and staff*. The supply and demand in college coaching is immensely disproportionate due to the limited number of coaching positions and the perception of how amazing it would be to have the opportunity to coach as a full-time job. Almost every youth coach in America has dreamed about joining the college or professional ranks. Athletic directors (AD) have a limitless supply of potential candidates to choose from should the AD decide to make a coaching change. There are only 345 D1 men's basketball coaches, 340 D1 women's soccer coaches, and 200 coaches in men's soccer. Head D1 coaches make up .004% of the American workforce. On the other hand, most professions have far more job opportunities. Let's take nursing as an example. There are about three million registered nurses working in this country. In banking—almost 2 million people are employed by FDIC insured commercial banks in the U.S. In college and professional athletics, coaches are under a microscope because there are so few of them relative to the population. If a coach cannot engage their staff and players, the results will be poor on field/court performance, a lack of development, negative feedback in athlete exit interviews and an increase in players transferring or quitting. In athletics, you are under immense public scrutiny, and the entire community—not just your employer—is well aware of your teams performance. In the business world, many of these negative factors can be hidden from the view of outsiders. Depending on the sport, college coaches are fired at a rate of 300%-900% greater than the average U.S. employee. I survived and thrived for over two decades in college coaching in large part because of my exceptional ability to engage my athletes and staff and to build an outstanding culture. Coaches who cannot engage those around them are out of the business rather quickly and often never return.

The answer to how to engage employees can be found by following a formula I have created based on personal and observed techniques that elite coaches use to achieve exceptional results. That formula is $E=MC^4$. No, it's not one of Einstein's equations.

INTRODUCTION

In 1905, Albert Einstein developed the theory of special relativity, $E=MC^2$. If you like physics, it's probably very fascinating. If you don't, trying to wrap your head around these simple letters can be an exhausting foray into an intellectual abyss. Bottom line, the theory of relativity says that the laws of physics are the same everywhere. Similarly, the laws of engaging people, whether it be my student-athletes and staff, or your employees, are the same everywhere. For my twist on $E=MC^2$, we will change the 2 to a 4 and end up with $E=MC^4$. The "E" stands for "Engagement." We will break down the other letters throughout the book. The best part about my formula is that it has nothing to do with time, space or mass, and you don't have to be a scientist or have an IQ in the gifted range to discern its application. After dissecting $E=MC^4$ I will move on through other engagement slayers and provide useable solutions to help you recover your rightful place among the most attractive places to work.

While we could define employee engagement from multiple sources, you know it when you see it. An employee who goes above and beyond, comes to work with a positive attitude, embraces the vision of the business, and is emotionally committed to its core values are all examples of what engagement looks like.

Why should employee engagement be at the top of your list of priorities? For businesses that exist to make profit, one answer is: Because disengagement (we will use disengaged and non-engaged interchangeably) is costing American businesses BILLIONS of dollars per year. In its simplest form, this is due to a lack of production from disengaged employees. There is a cumulative negative effect non-engaged employees have on poor customer experience, and on the costs associated with lousy talent retention.

In sports, those same attributes that make up an engaged employee can be found in engaged team members. Our "customers" are the fans who attend games. They are also the sponsors who pay universities and professional sports franchises millions of dollars a year to advertise their products. If you have a disengaged sports team, it will inevitably perform poorly and the fans won't keep coming to games; season ticket sales will drop, and advertisers will not renew their sponsorships with the teams.

Keeping employees engaged can be challenging. If they don't feel valued, don't see or understand the company vision and culture, are not empowered or challenged, they will disengage on some level.

In college athletics, we have all those challenges, and then some. There are walk-ons or low scholarship players putting in the exact same work as a full scholarship teammate who is "earning" $55,000 per year (the cost of tuition, room and board at the last school I was employed). The "pay gap" between those two players who put in the same time and commitment can be disengaging for some of the low or non-scholarship players.

The additional challenges we face running an athletic team are many. You know how the attitude and irritability levels change when the air conditioning goes out in your office and the temperature rises to 80 degrees inside? People get annoyed, are more easily irritated, and work production drops. In outdoor college sports, it's not uncommon for the artificial turf, which more than half of colleges have, to reach 130 degrees in August. Try capturing your employees' engagement in that setting. When was the last time an employee was made to work so hard in the office that they vomited? Stop by a college or professional team's practice in the preseason heat and see it firsthand during conditioning exercises. Coaches can have an exceptionally challenging time obtaining engagement with the additional factors in play that most businesses do not have to deal with. A "day at the office" for athletes often involves grueling physical conditioning. How many times a week are your employees literally screamed at, not just by bosses but by their own co-workers? Rarely, would be my guess. Observe a college practice and you will see teammates yelling at each other, adding to the emotional duress they are already under and presenting an obvious opportunity to disengage or turn off.

Our outdoor "office" can also be in the single digits during late fall and winter. It's the coaches job to keep the athletes engaged despite of some brutal outside forces. As a coach, I remember coming into the locker room at halftime of the America East Tournament final. The game was being played at the University of Vermont in November. We were down 4-0 to #8 in the country, the University of Hartford. When I entered the locker room to deliver my message, I saw multiple players crying. I assumed it was because they were upset being down so badly at halftime. As I started my positive message about the game and the score and to "keep their heads up," a captain interrupted me and explained the players weren't crying because of the score, rather they "couldn't feel their feet" as the temperature was in the low twenties that afternoon. Try engaging a group of players, down 4-0 against one of the best teams in the country, in twenty degree temperatures, who are so cold they are crying!

During a trip to play the University of Montana, eighty percent of our team came down with food poisoning the night before the game. Of the twenty players on the trip, ten felt they could try to leave their hotel beds to play the match. One initial problem was that a soccer game takes place with teams of eleven players on the field. Our ten brave souls arrived at the field and most didn't even attempt to warm up. Few had the energy to do so, because of the effects of the food poisoning and the horrific night before. Right before kickoff, we took the field, and within a few minutes we were down to nine players when one dropped to all fours and started dry heaving on the field. It was clear the game was over fifteen minutes in when we were already down several goals and had no energy to compete. We finished the afternoon with eight players, losing 6-1. God bless them, they truly stayed engaged until the final whistle.

I give you this background to help you understand that there are some great takeaways from my career that can be applied to employee engagement anywhere. Increasingly more businesses are using "team" and "coach" as part of their daily vernacular, but they rarely have members of their organization who have actually spent significant time in the world of athletics. It's in vogue to use these terms from sports but often, the people leading the movement have no background from which to apply the principles from athletics.

Coaches have a unique environment to create a special kind of commitment. From small schools to Fortune 500 companies, the principles of $E=MC^4$ will work to create a thriving workplace. In this book, you will find an in-depth approach guaranteed to help you improve employee engagement. The best part is that it is NOT an arduous, sophisticated, or laborious process. For many of you, it will come instinctively as you learn the formula. For others, it may not come as naturally with your management style, but rest-assured, you will still be able to learn and apply it quickly.

I do need to issue a brief disclaimer. If you are the prototypical "old school" manager or coach who believes employees just need to "suck it up," this book will probably be lost on you. If you can embrace just a bit of receptivity to change and acknowledge that there may be a better model out there, I assure you I can change your business and give you the chance to become exceptional.

PART 1

WINNING TEAMS

Before we start breaking down engagement, let's first agree upon some traits shared by both winning teams and successful programs.

- Good players (I did not say "great" players. While winning programs often have some exceptional team members, they rarely have the best players in the country in every position on the field or court).

- Engaged players and coaches

- Great culture

- A strategy and plan to implement that strategy

- Great leadership in Tier 1 (coach) and Tier 2 (players)

- Teamwork

- A shared goal or vision

- A strategy to achieve that goal or vision

- Investment

MATTER

The "M" in the $E=MC^4$ equation is MATTER. In athletics, to *realize* or *earn* engagement, the first objective is to make sure your athletes and staff understand they MATTER, or are valued, beyond just based on how high of a performer they are on your team. In sports, if an athlete feels that you, as the coach, only value them because of their athletic contribution, many will disengage immediately, especially those who are not star performers. My athletes—your employees—need to feel valued beyond just what they contribute to the bottom line. In most cases, the employees—or athletes—who "matter" the most are the ones who are the highest performers. There is nothing inherently wrong with this unless the rest of the team isn't recognized for the value they add. If I have a roster of 30 and only the top scorers or the starting 11 are really valued, many of the other 19 players will disengage. If some or all 19 disengage, the top 11 will most likely see their improvement and development diminish because they are not being pushed each day in practice by their teammates. Players need to know they matter beyond their talent. For your employees, this could be that they are recognized for leadership qualities, for a great ability to collaborate with others, for truly embracing the pillars and values of the company, or for their outstanding communication skills. That said, if a player is on your team, it should be because they add value. If they no longer add value and you cannot coach value out of them, then it is probably time for them to move on.

This is the area where recognition, rewards, and appreciation come into play. Publicly recognize employees for a job well done. If there were other team members involved in a successful outcome, be sure to include them. The athletics analogy would be for a forward who scores a great game-winning goal. Savvy coaches will praise the defender who won the ball to start the play, the midfielder who connected a great pass to the scoring player, and the other forward who followed the game-winning shot in case it was deflected. Consider showing appreciation for an employee who may not have achieved the result they wanted but their effort and process was praiseworthy. Don't confuse this with "everyone gets a trophy." For those of you not familiar with the youth athletics arena, the aforementioned reference is about a new generation of sports where there are no losers. Everyone gets a pat on the back regardless of ability or performance, and some youth leagues don't even keep score. Similarly, don't confuse this with "false praise." If an employee failed in all aspects of the sale, the deal, or the presentation, you should not verbally reward them.

Consider establishing a formal recognition program. For businesses with less than one-hundred employees, you can probably run it in house. For larger companies, you may want to consider hiring an outside organization that specializes in creating a platform for all types of staff recognition, incentives, and rewards. They have everything from large catalogs of merchandise to choose from to software that lets an employee send another employee a virtual greeting card with a message of appreciation. Do not start any program without thought and discussion about what it will look like and how it will be measured. There are plenty of resources out there to help you put this type of enterprise together. Recognition fuels positive engagement.

Your business exists to achieve success but there are times when specific failures are necessary steps toward a future success. The process becomes more important than the results. I know, some of you are cringing at that statement. Stay with me. I spent seven years coaching at Butler University and overlapped all those years with Brad Stevens (2 National Championship games as Butler basketball's head coach, NCAA records for most wins in a coach's first three years, second-youngest head coach to make the NCAA National Championship game, Boston Celtics head coach...more on Brad later). "I'm not focused on being results-oriented, I'm more focused on the process and the progress," Stevens once said. On the soccer field, I wanted to recognize and reward behaviors that were fundamental to our future success even if we failed to win a given game. I wanted other players to see and hear that praise to inspire them to model those same actions.

In a small organization, I feel you need to be cognizant of who you are openly praising and how often. The reason many managers don't publicly praise or publicly reward an employee is that they are concerned about how other employees may feel for not being recognized. In a small organization, everyone knows everyone else's business. If you have good employees, you should be able to find "wins" for all, or almost all members of your team over the course of a quarter or a year. The top performers will of course be recognized or rewarded more often. "Old school" managers may be wincing as they are reading this, thinking, "They are paid to do a good job, I'm not going to praise them for that." This kind of thinking simply no longer works. Today's generation responds differently. Are you trying to get the most out of your employees, which ultimately will help your business? Or are you trying to draw archaic lines about people who should "just do their job"? We aren't talking about praising them for showing up on time or closing a basic sale. We are talking about something that lines up significantly with your organizational vision. It could be small, like great customer service feedback from a client or something larger done by an entire team or division. Rewarding the entire team or department when one member does something special is another angle of recognition that can help build teamwork. It will subconsciously encourage other members of the team to work more selflessly. The "everyone wins" mentality.

The second part of "value" or "matter" is making sure the employees regularly see and understand the value that the organization provides its customers or community. Relate positive stories from clients or impactful changes made due to your company's products. Within this sphere is also where **purpose** can be recognized. People work harder and are more engaged if they feel what they are doing has a sense of purpose. It is definitely easier for employees to see the value of the company if the business is developing drugs that treat cancer or if you run an orphanage. The challenge is for the thousands of businesses that don't provide a service or product that is easily associated with making the world a better place or that do not have a natural employee engagement motivator built in. For example, some people who work in finance may be driven to perform at a high level because they enjoy helping others achieve their financial dreams. But there are plenty who operate in that same industry who are motivated by the built-in driver—the monetary windfall from success. For those who work in sports, they may or may not be motivated by doing their part to enhance the fan and community experience that comes with a successful team. What motivates many of them is being part of something that has a natural energy and excitement built into the daily job. Personally, working in college athletics, there was a constant energy year-round. Four of the five universities I worked for had elite basketball programs. When soccer was out of season, the buzz around the basketball season was a frenzied obsession by staff and fans alike. I believe that energy drove all of us to enjoy working hard.

If your business is something like manufacturing nuts and bolts to sell to the big box stores, you will most definitely find it more challenging to engage employees. There is no obvious/clear vision of how your products enhance lives by which employees find motivation. Forcing a steel rod through a series of dies at high pressure to form a bolt probably isn't that exciting after the first few days on the job. One of the most vital positions also happens to be one of the most mundane—quality control. It's easy to see how someone inspecting each bolt as it comes down the line could have an extremely low level of interest and engagement. It should also be obvious how one employee could financially destroy the company should they regularly allow flawed bolts to be packaged and sold. The big box store they sell to will eventually drop their line of product because of customer complaints.

Due to the lack of obvious value our bolt manufacturing business has, we need to create value outside of the business's mission statement. We need to create value by building a culture and an environment people want to be a part of. One of the most well-meaning but somewhat ineffective practices employed by thousands of businesses attempting to actualize a good culture revolves around predictability. Many companies hand out quarterly bonuses that are not at all related to the business's success during that period. Employees simply come to expect this and do not associate it with a reward for their hard work, their value, and commitment. A staff lunch is provided the Wednesday before Thanksgiving. A Secret Santa gift exchange happens in December. People come to expect these things; therefore, they lose some, not all, of their value. If you employ these practices, definitely keep doing them, but add some creativity and spontaneity to these traditions. When an employee closes a big sale, consider rewarding the entire team with a small bonus, gift cards or bring in a food truck for lunch. If you receive some great customer service feedback, order lunch in that week for the staff. Inspire your team with positive feedback from customers or anonymous testimonials from employees about another employee. Assuming it's feasible for your business operations, close early one Friday after a big "win" or great week. Better yet, as the boss, tell your team you will stay to answer the phones and wrap things up. Having staff see the boss sacrifice something so that the employees can reap a benefit is powerful.

When I coached college soccer and we were on a road trip, I would often collect the players' laundry after the Friday night game and wash/dry whatever they needed me to that night. For most teams, a young player, assistant coach, or team manager would take this duty on. Having your team see you embrace the duties that are ostensibly below you shows them that they matter. This is all scalable. If you are the president of a company with 50 employees, you would strategically approach these ideas a little differently than if you had 10,000 on the payroll, but the same general strategy can be applied.

Another driving force, especially for businesses that operate in the mundane, is HOPE. Hope for advancement, hope for a pathway forward, or hope for building a better life. Does your model provide hope? Are there visible examples of employees who have grown into more fulfilling positions? Do you know what the people under you want from their careers? Do you know what their goals are? Do you know what THEY believe their strengths are? Do you know what motivates them? An alarmingly high number of managers answer 'no' to these questions. Why? Because they don't fully understand the first "C"—Communicate.

COMMUNICATE

There are two parts to workplace communication. The first revolves around effective, or in many cases ineffective, manager-to-employee **communication structure**. Picture yourself (as a manager or leader) at the center of a spider web (the hub). The silk rings you construct outward around you work as an information conduit. While there may be dozens of rings coming off your hub, representing different tiers of your organizational chart, a good leader builds significant communicative connections outward at least two or three rings deep. Using the college athletics spider web model, an athletic director (AD) will often have five to ten employees (depending on the size of the department) in ring number one. These are usually Associate Athletic Directors. On the second layer, there are ten to twenty staff, which include all the head coaches. The third layer could have another fifteen to twenty personnel. As each ring grows outward from the hub, the AD is relying on the prior rings to do *some* of his or her communicating. There are many ADs and CEOs whose communicative presence only extends one tier. The more rings you can connect with, the higher the likelihood of corporate-wide engagement. You don't need to have the same level of contact with the third ring as you do with your inner circle, but neglect them at your peril.

The second part of communication is the more obvious part: the **quantity and quality of conversations**. The first thing to do when assessing your communication from manager or leader to employee is to ask whether communication exists at the level necessary to cultivate a productive relationship. Is the amount and quality of that communication enough to build and sustain good rapport? During my collegiate coaching career, I worked for different athletic directors (managers) who covered the communication spectrum from poor to excellent. I think it's important to contrast these opposing styles, in order to share significant takeaways.

One athletic director communicated from the first day he was hired that he had an "open-door communication policy." Employees could come in anytime to speak with him. That was a good start but it never materialized. It was just a leadership cliché. Why? Because if you are going to offer a policy like that, you must follow it up by demonstrating the sincerity of such a policy. Simply announcing it is not enough. Prove that you mean it. Make sure your employees feel you truly are accessible. Great leaders do this by taking the initiative to open, and keep open, lines of communication. Additionally, they act on the employee concerns brought to their attention. Staff then feel listened to and heard. Good leaders and managers don't wait for an employee to stop by, they take a proactive approach and check-in with staff regularly. They assume correctly that oftentimes, subordinates may be intimidated by their manager or a senior employee. To be clear, these "check-ins" are not meant to peel back the onion on performance review. They are meant to build and fortify communication lines. The manager's goals are to establish a foundation of trust, show the employee you value them enough to take the time to check in with them, learn what motivates them, and leave the employee with a feeling that they matter beyond just their performance. When the difficult conversations inevitably need to take place, having built a solid communicative relationship will allow for a more productive outcome from those tough conversations.

Let's go back to the AD with the open-door policy. In the four years after announcing his open-door policy, he called me one time and stopped by my office twice. That's a total of three personal connections in four years. (Employees had one annual performance review each year as well. We will get into those later.) To put this in perspective, most quality ADs will reach out to their head coaches once every week or two. Keep in mind, this was a relatively small department in terms of the number of coaches and assistant directors. This AD had less than twenty personnel who should have been in the first two tiers of his communication organizational chart. I would venture to guess that no matter what business you are in, very few of you have ever worked for a boss who reached out to you less than one time a year.

Contrasting this, I worked for an AD at a major school with a department twice the size of the above example.

It would have been understandable if the women's soccer staff didn't see him very often. The department, and the school for that matter, relied heavily on income generated by basketball and football. ADs at these types of institutions are pulled in countless directions by donors, trustees, the school president, different departments on campus, and their own staff. But he made a point of being visible to the entire department. He would poke his head in assistant coaches' offices to ask how their week was going. He recognized the value of connecting and communicating and approached it with a true genuineness. He made the non-revenue sports (i.e., not basketball or football) feel valued. Coaches were expected to produce at a high level, but at no point did coaches feel their jobs were being threatened. This commitment to communication endeared him to all of us, from secretaries to head coaches. Everyone's desire to perform at their best was subtly fueled by these interactions with their leader. When he conducted a version of an end of year performance review, he always asked the question: "What can we do to help you be successful here?"

Contrast that performance improving motivator with what many managers use to fuel their employees' drive—fear. Fear of the consequences of failure. Fear of termination. Fear of being on the receiving end of an employer's wrath. These employees will do just enough to keep themselves from having to file for unemployment. They are often not inspired to grow, as growth requires challenges that inherently contain potential failure. For these employees failure can mean humiliation and furor from their direct report.

As with many athletic directors, they rely on their assistant ADs to have a more hands-on relationship with the coaches. The same model applies with presidents and CEOs in corporate America. This is perfectly acceptable to relieve the AD of some of their workload. It works, only if the AD still manages to find regular, personal moments to connect with their tier one and two staff. At many universities, the AD has a few coaches who report directly to him or her. These sports are almost always the high-profile ones like football or basketball. Thus, it becomes doubly important for the AD to ensure the sports that do not have the same perceived value as those top priority sports still feel valued. The best ADs have an appreciation for the significance of this and make a serious effort to connect and communicate with coaches and athletes from these teams. Presidents and CEOs must delegate leadership responsibilities to their inner circle, which often includes Vice-Presidents, CFOs, COOs, etc. Some stop there. Others recognize the importance of still connecting with those employees' in rings three or four of their spider web. Oftentimes, those employees value to the company is arguably greater than the tier one employees. The tier three and four staff are closer to the cogs that make the engine run. They are more connected with the workers who power the company.

The second part of the communication process is about *collecting*. Great managers and leaders communicate in part to collect information to make a connection. To collect information, you must be doing two things— asking the right questions and listening. As a leader, your goal in this collection phase of communication is to have employees feel "heard" as well as learning more about them. I make a distinction between listening and hearing. Listening is what happens when you speak to someone, and they nod up and down. Hearing is what happens when that same person takes what you have said and retains it or acts on it. Do you remember the names and ages of your tier one and tier two employees' children? This is assuming you have ever asked. Do you know what those employees are passionate about outside of the office? Have you ever "acted" on their passion, meaning have you ever brought something up to them that you saw on TV or read in the newspaper that related to that employee's interests? Through communication with employees, small but important details are revealed. These seemingly trivial grains of information are the building blocks of connecting. The collection location also plays a part. Bringing an employee into your corner office, sitting them down across from your desk and beginning to rattle off scripted questions may get you some of the information you are trying to collect, but your employee will probably be guarded and somewhat uncomfortable. A nonthreatening, receptive environment allows for better communication. Almost anywhere is better than in your office. Keep in mind that in today's corporate culture, there are areas management should not, or cannot be asking employees about. If you aren't sure, one guideline would be to watch the comedy TV show The Office. A basic rule of thumb, while hilarious, nothing office manager Michael Scott says while communicating with employees should ever find its way into your communication Rolodex.

In college athletics, the most telling sign coaches pick up on as to the leadership quality of their athletic director involves losses. It's easy for an AD to stand in the tunnel of a basketball arena after a big win slapping hands with elated players and coaches. Conversation flows effortlessly with congratulatory colloquialisms sliding off the tongue. What about after a gutting loss? Many ADs are nowhere to be found. Rarely is this due to the AD being angry about the loss. Most of the time, it's a reflection of their inability to communicate during an adverse, emotionally-charged moment. I worked for one AD who would hightail it for the parking lot at the final whistle if we lost but would stay to congratulate me if we won. Can you imagine an army sergeant leading his squad into a firefight only to disappear when he realized they were losing the battle? Oftentimes, ADs don't know what to do or say and hide behind thoughts like, "I don't want to bother my coaches after a loss." Head coaches are on an island after a loss. The players are usually distressed. The ones who didn't play are even angrier that they could have helped the team win but didn't get the chance. The fans and parents are upset. Much of this is directed at the coach. This island is a lonely place for the coach. They could use some solidarity especially from someone in a position of power. This is the time for the AD (or CEO in business) to be visible. The coach doesn't need a lecture right now. The coach doesn't need a "pick me up" talk. What they need is visible support. They need to know "we are in this together." These are the times where you can build your legend as the leader you want to become.

CONNECT

Remember all that communicating and collecting we did? Now, to apply it. Our second "C" in the $E=MC^4$ formula is Connect. If you have communicated well, you have already started the connection process with your employees, possibly without noticing. There are two parts to connecting. First, in the most basic sense, you are connecting by establishing good, open lines of communication. Employees, or even friends for that matter, are drawn to connecting with people who communicate well. The right communication implies INTEREST in someone else's life. We all know people who would rate themselves exceptional communicators because they talk a lot. However, the best communicators and connectors listen well.

College athletics has some outstanding transferable lessons in connecting. Recruiting is the lifeblood for college coaches. Fusing relationships with potential student-athletes and their families is paramount to coaching success. The red carpet is rolled out for these potential program changers. The carpet takes multiples forms. Impressive facility tours, meetings with important members of the school staff, and—when it used to be legal according to NCAA rules—grand welcomes in the form of message boards, banners, personalized game jerseys, and even decorated cakes with the athlete's name. This type of connecting is done with the goal of making the recruit feel special and wanted. It's all for naught though if the coaching staff cannot continue to connect as they communicate throughout the visit. Connecting does not mean pontificating about what a great athletic program the university has. Those parts are subtly woven into the conversation, but that is not where connections are built. They are built by creating a relationship based on listening. Shrewd coaches revisit comments the student-athlete made earlier. They remember and regularly use each family members name in conversation and show they are listening with their body language. Consider the following.

In the 1800's, Benjamin Disraeli and William Gladstone were competing for the position of the prime minister of the United Kingdom. Winston Churchill's mother, Jennie Jerome, had dinner with them and when asked about her impression of them, she replied, "When I left the dining room after sitting next to Gladstone, I thought he was the cleverest man in England. But when I sat next to Disraeli, I left feeling that I was the cleverest woman." Disraeli won the election, not because he was smarter or a better politician, but because he had a sincere ability to make other people feel valued and important through connecting.

Where many coaches fail (and similarly employers) is after the recruit matriculates. The red carpet is gone and the relationship growth stagnates. Instead of building deeper connections that will ultimately contribute to further success, the coach moves on to the next potential recruit. They put in all that work to secure the student-athlete's commitment, only to watch engagement and prosperity plateau and slowly recess. The coach or manager has unintentionally broken the trust of the individual. The athlete or employee believed in the connection and that was an instrumental part of why they chose to attend that university or work at that business. Most managers are completely unaware of their own negligence in failing to nurture the connection they constructed early in the relationship. The manager gets buried in the day to day of the business and all that comes with it. They have employees to manage, customers to keep happy, internal fires to put out, a board of directors to keep informed, as well as potential issues in their own personal lives. The results can be unintentional deprivation in terms of continuing to build connections with employees. A different way to look at it from the manager's view of interacting and connecting versus the employee's view comes from the coach/player model. If one of my college soccer teams had thirty players, that meant I had thirty relationships to cultivate every week. I had to find a way to try to connect with all of them every week. But, from the players' perspective, there was only one head coach. Thus, they only had one coach/player relationship to develop each week. Your employees who have never had a team/staff under them will probably not understand the reality of the manager's job. All that employee knows is what they feel and that is that the bond and connection established early on has faded to what can seem like indifference...and they are on their way to becoming disengaged.

The second piece of connecting is more tactical. During your daily or weekly interactions with employees, you should have picked up on details of their lives. A sick child, a significant upcoming athletic event your employee's daughter is participating in, a family vacation, a book they were reading or a recipe they were going to attempt. All very small and mundane to you but to your employee, significant. Without being invasive, a simple question to your employee about the outcome of the event will strengthen your connection. Think of those elementary follow-up questions or conversations as the superglue that binds the relationship. People will work harder for managers whom they feel care about and connect with them. It's the old Teddy Roosevelt adage, "Nobody cares how much you know until they know how much you care."

Hilton Hotels and Resorts—Ranked #1 on the List of 100 Best Companies to Work For in 2019—developed a three-day program for senior leaders that had multiple engagement enhancers built into it. The program is designed for upper management to experience integral components of the business that they may never see. This includes working in Housekeeping, Banquet Services, and Food and Beverage. Participating in the program allows senior leaders to connect with frontline employees who they would never ordinarily interact with. They come out of the program with additional credibility and can use it to make connections well outside of their tier one and tier two network.

Do you have a strategy to connect with each employee in the first few rings of your web each week or month? If your answer is yes, and you have a scheduled meeting in your office with each one of them every month, this is not an automatic means to connect. A monthly meeting for performance review, or coaching, is separate from connecting and building relationships. While not entirely mutually exclusive, the office meeting that you feel will help build a connection while also "managing" the employee rarely serves that dual purpose. Make these connection moments more casual than a scheduled meeting.

If you do not have a plan for connecting, consider developing one. In my world of college athletics, in addition to trying to find moments in the hallway outside of the locker room, or on the team bus, I would also try to connect a bit deeper on the calendar day that matched a player's jersey number. In soccer, we typically had numbers 1-30, depending on the roster size. For example, on September 1st, I would find a few extra minutes with the player who wore #1 on our team. If we were off that day, I would roll it forward and try to connect with players #1 and #2 on the second of the month. Another approach was to break our coaching staff up (we had myself and two assistants) and assign each coach several players for the week. The goal was for that coach to *connect* with their designated players. An additional strategy I used was to have each class (i.e., the freshmen, sophomores, juniors or seniors) over for dinner once during the season. While it was a group, it was small enough to connect with them individually as well.

Don't underestimate the importance of connecting during the onboarding of new employees. Also, do not confuse orientation with onboarding. A Gallup poll found that only 12% of new employees felt their organizations did a great job with the onboarding process. Having new hires feel connected to the people and to the business is a crucial part of retention and employee productivity.

In college athletics, we added an additional connectivity level for our incoming freshmen to ensure they didn't quit during preseason (worst case scenario) and to help establish and optimize their performance within the team. This was accomplished by assigning each freshman a sophomore or junior student-athlete. Freshmen naturally gravitate to each other. The problem with that is that while the other freshmen can provide emotional support, they are of little help when it comes to building connections with the other classes. Additionally, freshman cannot "show the ropes" to each other as none have been through the experience of "onboarding" onto a team. The fear of the unknown can paralyze a rookie and limit performance those first few weeks. To counter this, each freshman would have a veteran player who would sit with them at every meal, make sure they knew where to go for team meetings, answer any questions they had, help them figure out how and where to buy their books for classes, etc. The result was an acceleration of the ties that bound players to the program. The secondary positive effect this had was to further engage the veteran players who were assigned to freshmen. They took additional ownership in the program by having some responsibility for their newcomer. The same model can be applied to businesses.

One university I worked for had a version of that for new employees but in the case of my employment, the program just existed as a concept. The veteran employee who was assigned to me reached out once and I never met him face to face. If you are going to have a plan to assign a current employee to an incoming one, it needs to have structure. The goal would be to have the two parties connect at least twice a week for the first month. The two primary objectives would be to have the veteran make additional introductions and connections for the new employee as well as being a resource for the inevitable questions that arise during those first few weeks on the job. Typically, the new hire is walked from office to office on the first day by the manager, meeting everyone at once, and is then left to fend for themselves. Having a peer mentor to do a more thorough version of introductions over the first few weeks can make a big difference in the experience and engagement.

Perfecting the connecting piece of the process is an art. It comes naturally to some and is a struggle for others. For those mangers who discount connecting, this often means they simply aren't good at it and thus, avoid it by diminishing its value.

COACH

COACH is the third "C" in the formula. Athletic coaches and business managers share many of the same attributes. On paper, they can seem identical. Both *should* be good leaders, communicate very well, be motivators, and help people reach their goals. Since we are in the coaching section of the book, and since in my world, leadership and coaching are eternally linked, I am going to let you in on a secret about leadership. According to a Google search, there are over 15,000 books devoted to leadership. There is boundless information available—much of it good—on the most important characteristics of great leadership. But here is what exceptional leadership comes down to. Leadership is not about a position or a title; it is about relationships. Read that sentence again. Think about the people in your life who have been in a leadership position. Think back to high school and consider the team captains if you played a sport or the class officers in student government. Consider the managers or company presidents you have worked under during your career. Most likely, many of these folks looked at their leadership as it related to a title. *I'm the team captain, so you will do what I tell you...I am the Assistant Manager so you will listen to me...I am the president, so you will abide by my directives.* In my opinion, more leaders lead by position or title than by effectively building relationships. As I mentioned, there are dozens of traits that make up a great leader, but in terms of your own leadership or coaching upcoming leaders in your organization, the most important thing you can do is to recognize the mammoth value that **leading by building relationships** has over the traditional *title* or *position* approach.

If you want to witness the biggest difference between business managers and athletic coaches, attend a high-level sports team's practice. You will most likely see a passion for teaching as you watch the coaches interact with the players. This isn't just at the high school or college level. It exists at NFL and WNBA practices. Grown men and women are being coached and taught. As the practice unfolds, the game becomes part of the teaching environment. Instant feedback is provided as drills play out. Immediate opportunities to applaud or correct reveal themselves during these two-hour practice windows. Coaches don't wait until the "annual performance review" to provide feedback. A stern word here, a moment of praise there. The best practices unfold like choreographed dances. The coaches are not directing from an office behind a desk, they flow seamlessly on the court or field with the players. This is coaching, not managing.

Before we get any deeper into coaching, let's first identity the fundamental difference between *training* employees and *coaching* employees. For new hires who do not yet have the technical skills or understanding of their position, training is paramount prior to their coaching. For a manager to maximize the coaching effect, the person being coached must already have, or learn, the basic skill set for the job. This is where a plethora of businesses fail to give themselves the best opportunity to succeed. Training involves having a program that allows the transfer of knowledge for a given position within the organization. On the other hand, think of coaching more as augmenting a current skill set. It's taking someone with a degree of experience and enhancing their performance. For large corporations, new employee training programs are often comprehensive and well-structured. While possibly mundane at times for the new employee, the information transfer occurs on schedule and provides the employee a cornerstone from which to build a successful career. Smaller organizations often have less structured onboarding. Their new employee training lacks the necessary framework. Coaching someone who does not have adequate knowledge about their position is a frustrating proposition for any manager. The result is a partially-trained team member who is likely on course to join the 67% of disengaged employees. Does your organization provide thorough training? Do current employees in that position provide feedback on best practices for training that job?

Coaches plan practices in advance. They strategize with their staff and at times, with the players. They identify strengths upon which to build and glaring weaknesses that need to be fixed. Coaching staffs approach practices with a desired outcome goal. Every drill or exercise is methodically sequenced into the day. Each member of the staff has a copy of the practice plan. Usually, the plans are very detailed, even down to the exact number of minutes allocated to each drill. I used to post the day's practice on a wall at the field for all the players to see. It contained diagrams of the exercises as well as the purpose of the drills. This helped to provide a visual map of what the team's focus was going to be on that day.

How often do you, as a manager, start the week or the day with a "practice plan"? Do your employees know the direction of their focus for that day or week? Do you solicit feedback to create a plan?

Don't confuse what follows with that of the "SWOT" buzzword (strengths, weaknesses, opportunities, threats) commonly used among businesses. Typically, these are employed once every six months or so and are an important piece of business strategy. The potential problem with SWOT analysis is that there is often not a weekly plan built around the SWOT intelligence gained. The C-suite executives come away with useful insight from the analysis, but the information derived from it needs to be disseminated in the form of a weekly or daily "practice plan."

As you build your weekly "practice plans", consider four areas to break your pie chart into; strategies, new development, weaknesses, and competition. The largest section should always be over 50% of the pie and it should contain strategies to continue to build upon your strengths. These can be individual employee strengths as well as product or corporate mission strengths. Successfully separating your team from others comes down to building world-class strengths.

The second part of the chart will focus on new development. This could mean adding a new product line, expanding or improving areas of your business (that are not already key strengths) or it could concentrate on providing new tools to enhance employees' skill sets.

The third area would be attention to weaknesses. Not just general weaknesses, rather on those that will clearly hurt your bottom line if not corrected. Do not get carried away spending more time in this area than you absolutely need to. As you assess how much time and resources will be committed to each area of the pie, be wary of the trap of trying to improve all areas of your company where you see weaknesses. There isn't enough time in the week to do this and you will end up with a business that is average in every area. Additionally, think about trying to hide team weaknesses while you are working on improving them. Sports teams need to employ that regularly. As a college soccer coach, I had several outstanding center midfielders (the engine of the team) who were not overly mobile or athletic. Against opponents who deployed very athletic central midfielders of their own, we would subtly adjust our formation and play with an additional center midfielder to help defensively against these athletic opponents. We would essentially hide our weakness.

The final piece of the pie chart should center on the competition. Coaches are constantly preparing for the next opponent. They do this by collecting information and creating a scouting report. In business, this means preparing for the competition. Yes, the best teams and the top corporations may be good enough to do what they do very well and not worry about the competition. They may have world-class athletes or a product no one else has and they win on their own brute strength. But this is rare and fleeting. For most of us, this model isn't sustainable. Preparing to anticipate your opponent's strategies is paramount to your success. The Titanic had no competition. That is, until it realized it did— icebergs. The hubris of the vessel's leadership team was responsible for over 1,500 deaths. Kodak ruled the film market but leadership was resistant to change and the company failed to recognize competition would catch up if it didn't adjust. They filed for bankruptcy in 2012. Blockbuster video rentals dominated their market. Potential competition arrived in the form of Netflix, who even approached Blockbuster with a partnership. Blockbuster turned the proposal down. They underestimated Netflix's business model. In 2010, Blockbuster filed for bankruptcy and Netflix is now worth billions. I'm not suggesting you get so caught up in identifying potential threats from the opposition that you lose sight of your own practices and strengths. But being aware of competition will allow you to see potential threats as well as help stimulate new ideas for your own organization. I cannot speak for every sports organization, but I would venture to guess based on my twenty years in college athletics that it is an incredibly small percentage who do not commit some effort to assessing their competition.

Sports Team	Business Competitor
Competition's Key Strengths	(A) Prepare to defend against them (B) Learn from them to strengthen your business
Competition's Key Weaknesses	(A) To exploit (B) Learn from them to de-risk your business
Competition's Formation	Org. Chart/Structure (Is there a better or more efficient way for you to be structured?)
Competition's Style of Play (Is the opponent defensive/ offensive minded, aggressive...)	Does your style of play (sales, marketing, processes...) allow you to adapt to the ever changing competition?
Top Players	Best Products/Best People
Game Plan	Do you have any new business strategies based on your "scouting reports"?

WHAT information and how MUCH information a coach shares with their team from the scouting report is critical. As a coach, you are not trying to overwhelm or intimidate your team with the report. A good scouting report is still about YOUR team and what YOU are going to do to be successful. The same goes for a business. Even if you are "scouting" Google, you aren't trying to become Google. You are trying to learn from them, identify weaknesses, and possibly incorporate some aspects into your business.

There is a second scouting report worth discussing— your customer. Most companies do some degree of homework on their customer prior to meeting with them or launching a new product. It is certainly easier for a business that has a large budget and access to unlimited data and technology to understand a potential customer on something much deeper than a superficial level. Many businesses do not have the resources to look at a customer's makeup and needs at the granular level. We can take that same scouting report above and apply it to the customer to improve our odds of acquiring and retaining clients and consumers.

Your Business Assesses	Application to Customer
Customer's Key Strengths	Can you help your customer enhance those?
Customer's Key Weaknesses	Can you help improve those weaknesses or help hide them?
Customer's Formation/Top Players	Who in their organization is the decision maker for buying your product?
Game Plan	Based on this information what approach gives you the best opportunity to win/ retain that customer?

Once a sports team has built a scouting report, they practice the offensive and defensive plays that will be implemented based on their game plan. The coach will organize what is called a "walk-through" a day or two prior to the game. This will simulate things they expect to see the opponent try to execute as well as strategies they themselves will employ. Walk-throughs are exceptionally choreographed. *If the opponent does this, we do that.* The players are learning how to respond to the fluid situation which will unfold during the game. Most high-level teams also incorporate visualization into the same type of training. Players are walked through a visualization exercise of how to respond when an opponent runs a certain play. Additionally, they visualize their own patterns and plays. The best businesses undertake a version of a pre-game walk-through when readying for a sales pitch or proposal. If the customer says *this*, we respond with *that*. Are your employees trained to deal with almost any situation or question that may emerge? I say "almost" because there will inevitably be a scenario that unfolds which may not have been predicted. Anticipating probable customer responses is accomplished by developing a scouting report.

The top organizations combine the scouting report on their competitors along with the report on the customer they are about to meet with. Why do they combine these reports? If you said it was because the company will craft a pitch that will appeal to the customer's need while subtly discounting what your competitors can do for them and enhancing what you can do, you would be right. In college athletics, potential recruits were our *customers* and other schools who were recruiting the same students were our *competitors*. When high school student-athletes came to campus for a tour and visit, we had a scouting report for much of our recruiting competition (other schools that student was considering) and one for our customers—the student-athletes.

You don't need to have all four sections of the pie chart accounted for each week. There may be weeks where your focus is only on three of the four areas. But always have a piece dedicated to enhancing your strengths.

This is the anatomy of weekly practice plans across the country in college and professional sports. It is a model that has worked at all levels, including for national championship caliber teams.

What did you see? Great coaches ask that question to point guards and quarterbacks alike after an errant pass or turnover. The game presented a scenario and the player made a decision. Instead of "managing" the player by telling them which pass should have been made, players are "coached," which is just a conversation about what they saw and why they chose the option they did. Coaches understand that there may have been four or five choices the quarterback or point guard had at that moment. The key is to have the player figure out which choice would have been great, which one was poor and which would have been OK. Good coaches don't decide that every time for the athlete. They allow the player to work through the different options. Managers often tell their employees exactly what the scenario called for. They aren't training employees to make decisions; they are training them to be robots regurgitating preprogrammed information. In some roles, this may work fine, but in today's competitive business environments that are in constant flux, coaching people to think critically is paramount.

CULTURE

The final letter in our $E=MC^4$ equation is another "C." Executives often talk about **culture**, but they cannot give you a concrete plan on how they create it and what they feel are the key components to outstanding culture. Do you have a great culture at your company? If so, what are its specific critical ingredients? What are the core values it is built around? Does your culture deliberately unfold according to your plan or does it evolve by accident? If you had to think about your answers or if you found yourself improvising a response, you are part of the majority. Not to worry, a culture plan can be created.

Whether you realize it or not, your business has a culture. Remember our leadership spider web analogy? The further removed you are from the people working in the outer rings, the less likely you are to have any idea what the culture is. You may *think* you know what it is. Head coaches rely on assistant coaches, team leadership groups, and team captains to keep their thumb on the culture pulse. Assistant managers, shift supervisors, and battle-scarred employees can all fill the same role.

If you spend enough time around the world of NCAA D 1 collegiate athletics, you will hear the word *family* used when describing a particular athletic department or team culture. Read almost any press release from a college athletic director who is announcing a new hire and you will undoubtedly hear them welcoming the newest employee to the *family*. While there are athletic departments that truly meet the description of what many of us would agree to be a family, most do not. A healthy well-adjusted family loves and supports you unconditionally. You can confide in and trust family members. Family members have long-term commitments to each other. The current culture in many athletic departments is to support the coaching staff—**if they are winning**. The love and support is completely conditional. Coaches develop skeptical trust of their universities because they have seen so many of their peers blindsided by administrations who preach family but then decide to "go another direction" with coaches, who by many accounts have often been successful. On the rare occasion a coach is given a long-term commitment in terms of a contract, there is no commitment. There is just a buyout. If the coach underperforms (a subjective word in athletics), the administration simply fires the coach and pays out the remainder of the contract. Or worse, the university tries to find a reason to fire the coach and void the contract "for cause" which would potentially relieve them of paying out the contract. That's not remotely close to meeting the true definition of commitment.

Corporate America also misuses *family* regularly. If you are using the word to describe your culture, be sure that it meets the accepted definition. If not, then change the word. It is completely fine if your organization wants to build a great culture but is not comfortable using "family" to describe it. You are far better being honest with your employees about what the culture expectation is than by using hollow words and phrases that will end up undermining your attempts to build a great culture. Let your people know what your organization stands for and what you will do to support that culture. Then, back it up. If you do not, you will lose trust, which is the beginning of the end for many businesses. Culture is one of the few things you have total control over in your business. If people are not embracing the culture, you can move them on.

Human Resources and those involved in the recruiting and interviewing process should know what the culture expectation is. In college coaching, I didn't have any "middle-men" involved in the vetting and recruiting of a prospective student-athlete. This was a very good thing. It was difficult for an individual to slip through the cracks and end up on our team who was not a good fit for our program's culture. In large organizations, it can be challenging to filter out the prospective employees who will not be a good fit with the culture. The three keys to this are first to make sure HR, as well as the hiring managers, CLEARLY understand the types of personalities that will fit the culture. Second, the culture expectations must be communicated up front in the recruiting/hiring process to the potential new team member. The mistake many coaches and managers make is to tell the player or job candidate what they want to hear to close the deal because the recruited individual appears very talented. The person may accept a scholarship or job offer but there is now a big problem—you have someone who is either going to need to be changed to fit into your culture or the business itself will need to change to accommodate the employee. While every person can be managed differently based on their skill set, what motivates them, and their disposition, applying a completely different set of culture rules to certain employees is a slippery slope. You are usually far better off losing a recruit who self-selects out of the process because they don't buy into your expectations or culture, rather than bringing in someone who clearly is not a fit. Third, you need to be able to assess the risk versus reward of hiring someone outside the box. If the reward could be huge and the collateral damage minimal of bringing on this person, maybe you take the chance. If you do this, you need to be willing to cut your losses before they corrupt the culture if things go sideways.

Great culture doesn't just happen. It is calculated by the coach or manager and based on prioritized values. Behaviors outside of the accepted values must be corrected immediately. The culture needs to be protected at all costs. It is what spurs the behavior, and **the behavior is what ultimately produces the results**—positive or negative.

Creating the culture is a fluid science. It can vary based on the mentality of the leadership and the category of the business. A mom and pop hardware store may have a different culture vision than that of an investment bank. Or, they could both employ the same culture principles. Some businesses thrive on a cutthroat model where the culture is "eat or be eaten." Individual wins are mounted like a trophy hunt for all to see, while the stragglers are ostracized. Other businesses have proven track records of success applying a much more nurturing culture model. As long as employees know what the model is, it's their choice to join that culture. You can find examples of all kinds of cultures that work, but I believe there are some core components the BEST environments share, which check two boxes—successful performance and unequivocally positive employee experiences. If one of your primary goals is employee engagement, which in turn will drive success, positive experiences are an integral part of it.

You could find dozens upon dozens of words and phrases that are important to culture. I have created my own acronym using what I feel are the key components to establishing a great culture.

Creativity	Businesses that cannot or will not change will fail. Creativity drives positive change. Encourage it.	Stop saying 'It won't work' to new ideas. Figure out how they might work.
United Vision	You must have a united vision, not just management's vision. Employees should be involved and on board. Additionally, the corporate hierarchy must be structured to encourage daily unity among ALL staff.	Does your company's vision/mission statement make sense? Do you have a yearly vision (sub-mission statement) that is created from employee feedback/communication? Are the executives visible and interacting on a daily basis with everyone from vice-presidents to warehouse workers?
Liable	People should know the standards and be accountable for not meeting them.	In the hiring process this should be made clear. If the accountability is stated in such a way that it appears to be threatening, re-work it.
Team	Celebrate team wins. Encourage collaboration.	Are employees incentivized to work for themselves or to collaborate? Are bonuses only individual or also team based?

Useful Debate	Conflict is a necessary part of growth. Encourage it.	Do your staff meetings have conflict and debate? Does the debate stay within predefined boundaries?
Relevant	If management doesn't truly value employees, your culture model will not matter and you will not generate optimal business success.	How do you show value? Is it primarily/ only based on an employee's bottom line production?
Empower	Encourage and recognize contribution. This feeds ownership which in turn improves job satisfaction.	Do you provide employees autonomy in their work?

Creativity

According to the most recent World Economic Forum report—which polled leading global employers on the top skills they were looking for in new employees—**Creativity** rose dramatically and was ranked #3 on the list. Google had a famous '20% time' policy where employees were encouraged to spend 20% of their work week engaged in activities that could benefit the company but that were outside the scope of their regular weekly projects. Regardless of how many employees used this model to help generate new ideas, the outside the box thinking was a brilliant way for Google to show how they valued creativity. They took the adage, "be creative" and gave it structure. Once you decide how to implement creativity, the next step is how to share those new ideas. In its most basic form, creative ideas can be shared via the "suggestion box." The large-scale version is the full-day Corporate Creative Sharing Retreat, and there are multiple platforms in between.

Once the idea sharing format is established, be cautious with your first response to many of these ideas, which is often, "This will never work." Decades of experience in the industry can work against managers when new ideas are presented. There can be a subconscious internal bias against novel ideas that come from divergent thinking. If you truly understand the value of creative employees and their ideas, you need to make sure they feel heard and considered. Many suggestions will eventually end up in the proverbial shredder. How they get to the shredder is meaningful. A surefire way to end creative contributions is to asphyxiate them before they even have life breathed into them. Do not confuse this with feeling the need to wear kid gloves so as not to hurt an employee's feelings when shooting down an idea. While everyone would love all their suggestions to be implemented, first and foremost, the team member just wants to be heard and considered.

Have you ever heard of Blue Ribbon Sports? Most have not. But you probably have heard of the company that Blue Ribbon became—NIKE. Creativity helped revolutionize the running shoe industry. Founder Bill Bowerman developed a shoe sole, which has now been in existence for decades. Just about every running shoe made today has its roots in Bowerman's 1971 creative epiphany. He was sitting at the breakfast table while his wife made waffles and he had the sudden inspiration to pour the liquid material that composed his company's shoe sole into the waffle iron. The legend goes he was so excited about the idea that he forgot to spray the waffle maker with a non-stick solution and ruined the waffle iron. Bowerman immediately went to the store and purchased several more to experiment with the sole. The rest is history. Nike still makes a version of their Waffle Trainer shoe today.

Check your current culture. Do you want creativity? Are you rewarding employees who don't make mistakes and punishing those who do? If so, you are encouraging actions and behaviors that are risk averse—meaning you are killing creativity—possibly without knowing it. There is a time and place for creativity, whether it be in sports or in business. A football coach probably does not want the offensive coordinator to call an overly creative play involving multiple laterals close to their own goal line due to the risk-reward scenario. As a soccer coach, I didn't want my defenders trying something tricky in front of their own defensive goal. In business, you may not want your accounting department to run wild with "creative accounting." Don't confuse creativity with a lack of planning. "Winging it" right before a sales pitch with an idea that hasn't been vetted and worked through isn't the kind of creativity we are talking about.

United

Next on the list is the word **United** which will have two parts. First, the company mission and vision need to be united ambitions. While these two words are often used interchangeably, I look at mission as why your company exists, its purpose, and its strategy. Your vision is more aspirational. It is what the company wants to be and the impact it will have on a grand scale. You can have two separate statements or combine them into one if you are just starting out down the mission/vision road. Mission and vision must be something the cleaning crew, the delivery drivers, the secretaries, and the C-suite executives all can UNDERSTAND and BELIEVE in. It should be something that bonds through shared emotion. It should be simple, not too wordy, specific to your industry, realistic, and separate your business from your competitors. Let's look at Patagonia's mission. They are an American outdoor clothing company that does almost 1 billion dollars a year in sales. Additionally, they donate 1% of all sales to the preservation and restoration of the natural environment. Their statement: *Build the best product, cause no unnecessary harm, use business to inspire and implement solutions to the environmental crisis.* The average Patagonia employee rating on Glassdoor is 4.3 out of 5 (5 being a great company to work for), compared to the average company rating on Glassdoor of 3.3. Two of Patagonia's closest competitors scored 3.3 and 3.7, a significant difference from Patagonia's 4.3. The CEO based in California and an hourly

Patagonia employee working at a mall in Ohio could both embrace the mission statement. While the two people would probably never meet, they are united through the mission.

If we look at Apple Inc., it's difficult to find a ubiquitous mission statement. They have multiple statements and visions and a much different approach than that of Patagonia. Below are two separate statements. They are not listed together on any Apple site.

1. *To bringing the best user experience to its customers through its innovative hardware, software, and services.* This statement is concise and fits with what I believe a mission statement should look like.

2. *We believe that we are on the face of the earth to make great products and that's not changing. We are constantly focusing on innovating. We believe in the simple not the complex. We believe that we need to own and control the primary technologies behind the products that we make, and participate only in markets where we can make a significant contribution. We believe in saying no to thousands of projects, so that we can really focus on the few that are truly important and meaningful to us. We believe in deep collaboration and cross-pollination of our groups, which allow us to innovate in a way that others cannot. And frankly, we don't settle for anything less than excellence in every group in the*

company, and we have the self-honesty to admit when we're wrong and the courage to change. And I think regardless of who is in what job, those values are so embedded in this company that Apple will do extremely well. This statement seems to combine a mission and a vision along with an "About Us" statement found on many business websites. While powerful, an employee would be hard-pressed to recall and regurgitate all of this.

The third illustration I will use is that of the Steamboat ski resort in Colorado. Steamboat is regularly ranked as one of the top ten ski resorts in the U.S. On their website, you will not find a mission statement but you will see a Culture Guide. The guide answers four questions. *Why do we exist? What is most important? What do we value? How will we behave?* Each question has a concise answer (about six words). Customers and employees alike can look at the guide and understand exactly what Steamboat stands for and what it expects to deliver.

You need to decide what will inspire and unite your employees when you look at mission and vision statements—or Culture Guides—as well as choosing how often those are altered or supplemented with new thoughts. While the statement can change, it is not something you would want to do regularly. Being fickle about who you are and what you do will not help build trust with your customers. Something you can do annually is to add a "sub-mission." Is there a specific focus or theme your business wants to commit to for that calendar year? Have you asked for and received feedback from employees on themes or initiatives they would like to see implemented? It is also an opportunity for employees in separate divisions to cross-collaborate and unite around one annual drive. This has the additional positive effect of letting staff know that their voices have been heard.

While my college teams had some expectations and pillars which did not change, we did employ the concept of sub-missions. One year, *the team decided* they wanted to commit regularly to a certain homeless shelter. Most athletic departments either require or strongly encourage their teams to give back to the community, but this usually takes the form of volunteering once per semester. The university sends a photographer and the pictures are splashed on the school website with a story about how wonderful it is that the team is giving back. The problem is that these aren't true missions. They are often one-time public relations opportunities. The year we worked with the shelter, our players organized a group to make the trip downtown **every** Wednesday night during the spring. That commitment and experience was unquestionably more uniting than the typical one-hit wonder give backs.

Like sub-missions, each year we had an annual theme for our team. One year, it was "The Journey." I told the following story about the theme's origin in my book *Cope, Rise, Thrive!* In 1999, I was hired by Butler

University to take over their women's soccer program. A year later, Butler men's basketball hired a volunteer assistant coach who had decided to leave a successful job at Eli Lilly to chase his dream. This was potentially a huge financial and career risk if it did not work out for him. The basketball volunteer gradually rose through the ranks and in 2007, he had worked his way up to head coach. In his first season, Brad Stevens led the Bulldogs to 30 wins, becoming the third-youngest head coach in NCAA Division I history to have a 30-win season. In 2010, he took Butler to its first modern-day national championship game, losing at the buzzer to Duke. The following season, he achieved the improbable. Butler was back in the national final. I remember seeing an interview the night before the 2011 championship game. The reporter asked him something about whether the season would be a failure if they didn't win this year, after having come so close the past season. I'll paraphrase here, but Brad told the interviewer that his season's success wasn't about whether they won or lost the following evening. He said it was about *the journey*. We chose The Journey as a theme one season because as much as winning is paramount at the D1 level, the highs, lows, positive, and negative experiences are all part of the ride and you have no choice but to accept them as they come. Those moments, not just the result, are what make your journey special.

The second part of the word "united" has to do with how often the top brass amalgamate with employees several rungs down the corporate ladder. If your office layout isn't structured to have regular interaction with different tier employees, either change it, or encourage upper management to spend time each day around the people whose business cards—if they have them—may not have CEO, COO, CFO, VP, Manager, or Executive printed on them. The pushback you receive could be that your executives simply do not have enough time to do this. There are plenty of multitasking opportunities throughout the week. For example, the simple conversation a manager wants to have with a co-worker doesn't need to be conducted in the office behind a desk. Many of these can take place as you are walking through the hallway, warehouse, break room, accounting office etc., making what I call "micro connections" with potentially dozens of other employees. Visible leadership is uniting. In the "Connect" chapter, I illustrated how Hilton has upper management participate in an intensive three-day immersion program. Senior leaders work alongside bellboys and wait staff, carrying luggage and serving drinks. Having the staff see upper management in the trenches is subtly powerful and sends a strong message of solidarity. Visible leaders who acknowledge each employee they pass on their daily circuit through the office is a uniting force. If your goal is the coveted World's Best Boss coffee mug, call them by name as they go by.

Liable

From the first interview to the last day on the job, employees should know your company standards and be accountable (**Liable**) if they do not meet them. If your culture is important—which it should be—the employees need to know exactly what it is and what is expected. The same goes for their job description and performance. *Accountability standards* is another way to think of the "L" part of your culture. There is a fine line between having standards come across as threatening versus delivering standards as a part of the culture everyone embraces. I worked with someone who turned down a job offer because at the end of the interview she was told if she was not at her desk every day by 7:59 she would be fired. Standards for timelines and work hours are necessary for most businesses but the communication of the requirement was poorly delivered. There is nothing empowering about threatening an employee's job with a statement like that. A second story comes to mind out of the coaching world. At a large holiday party for faculty and staff, a university president told the group that an 8-4 football record (8 wins, 4 losses) will get a coach fired at her institution. The expectation was 10-2. First of all, 8-4 is a significant accomplishment in the competitive world of college football. Second, this university was not blessed with the unlimited budget and resources a select few of the annual top performing football schools had. While 10-2 can be a wonderful stretch goal or vision for the program to chase, it's unrealistic for most schools to regularly win 10 games every year. That statement of liability was going to do nothing to positively impact the culture, nor would it affect any future results. NCAA D1 coaches are a special breed. They know there is pressure to win. They do not need a school president, who likely does not understand the job of coaching, to publicly threaten termination over what most would deem success (8-4). Since that president issued the statement, the program has had only one season in the past six that met her standard of success. During a three-year period following the president's statement, only 7% of all college Football Bowl Subdivision teams went 10-2 or better. Again, the president's expectation would have been a great stretch goal, but to tie it directly to a condition of employment is not only unrealistic but it creates a threatening environment, not one of empowerment. Yes, you might have some people realize success under a cloud of peril, but it is not sustainable in most cases.

Most businesses will have two types of accountability— personal and team. The personal one involves setting clear job descriptions, expectations, and consequences. Assuming you have competent employees, the common thread amid personal accountability failures is often a lack of clarity from the top. The prevalent issue among team accountability breakdowns is that while each person on the team needs to meet their given expectations, there still needs to be one recognized person on the team who is responsible for the team achieving its goal.

Team

The next word in the CULTURE acronym is **Team**. This probably requires the least amount of explanation. We have all heard the phrase "there is no I in team" and countless other versions of this expression. While hackneyed sayings like this pervade sports and corporate culture alike, they do have merit. Some businesses and teams can ride a single individual to championship levels but it is not a sustainable model. The elite performer can expand the team or business by a number greater than one if they understand the multiplier that is collaboration. Within *team* should be an expectation of how we want to treat each other. The expected and acceptable peer to peer and manager to employee behaviors should be clear. Next, assess how often you are rewarding and praising team accomplishments versus just individual achievements. If teamwork is important to your culture, those successes should be acknowledged regularly. Creating an identity around the higher purpose of team will also add value and inspiration to individual employees' potentially banal day-to-day work. To use another sports analogy, your goal is to have employees who are playing for the name on the "front of the jersey" (the company name) not the name on the back of the jersey (the employee's name).

Useful Debate

Useful Debate is the next component of culture. All of us have probably sat in a meeting listening to an idea, concept, or product that, in our mind, has many flaws. Our inner dialogue goes through a checklist of how ridiculous and unsound the notion is. *Why doesn't someone say something?* you think. Saying something could be uncomfortable and hurtful, but that uncomfortable conversation is exactly how ideas grow into game-changing strategies and products. Harvard Business Review calls this type of necessary communication "creative friction."

The structure behind useful debate has two key components: First, it begins and ends with respect. The individual who proposes an idea that, by all accounts, is not practical or would damage the company may be the very person who down the road has a million-dollar idea. If they are silenced due to the perception of disrespect you may miss out on a brilliant future proposal.

"It is the mark of an educated mind to be able to entertain a thought without accepting it," said Aristotle. The key word to me in this quote is *entertain.* Remember, people want to be heard. This is the second element in the useful debate structure. You can entertain their idea, proposal, or solution without agreeing with it in the end. The feeling that they were at least listened to is a key component of useful debate. We have all sat in meetings where the period is not yet on the end of the sentence and the idea is squashed immediately. Unless you happen to be in the White House Situation Room during a potential massive threat, and time is of the essence, entertaining an idea is of no harm to anyone. Consider reverse engineering the thought through questions. Is there something behind the idea which could be the beginning of a useful strategy or proposal?

Discord and conflict are catalysts for growth and innovation. Maybe you don't have any of that friction and you're proud of what appears to be universal harmony on your team. If that is the case, you are one of a small percent of successful businesses that has no conflict—which is actually not a good thing. Or, more likely, you have your head in the sand. While a lack of conflict may appear to be a trait of a successful team that is operating in perfect accord, that lack of conflict probably means you have a group whose goal is to maintain the status quo. If no one is encouraged to think critically or challenge corporate strategies—which may lead to debate and discord—the business is not growing. You do, however, want to catch the creative friction among team members before it gets to disunity and dissension. The best outcome from conflict is collaboration, which leads to future success. We want the worst outcome to be: "we agree to disagree." If it devolves beyond that it often becomes personal, negative, or hostile. This is where potential business breakthroughs end. Your culture must be okay with conflict, provided everyone understands the rules: respect and entertain the ideas of others.

There is a parallel in sports. Turn on an NBA game and you will undoubtedly witness debate and conflict among teammates during the game. Athletics, like business, is competitive and competition often brings out heated dialogue. Preemptive strike number one is to build great relationships off the court so that players can better handle tempestuous moments during the game. Sports teams build these relationships among their players in a couple of ways. One way is to strategically room certain players together on road trips or seating them next to each other on team flights or bus trips. Conversations go well beyond cursory and this is where relationships are built. In soccer, the center defender would often be roomed with the goalkeeper or with the other center defender on trips. This is because these three needed to be able to communicate at an elite level under substantial pressure. The better their relationships off the field, the more effectively they could communicate on the field without shutting down under what could feel like a personal attack.

Striving towards shared common goals is another method by which relationships are constructed. Is your vision and mission understood by all? Do you have clear goals set? It is the "we are all in this together" mentality that helps tie different personalities together and build relationships.

Off-site team building exercises are commonly employed by all levels of sports teams in order to strengthen relationships so that when the pressure is increased, a referee (manager) isn't constantly needed to resolve a problem. Taking your team out of its normal working environment often provides a better setting to break down barriers and build these relationships. Make sure you remove the hierarchy structure for some of the team building activities. This means the CEO (coach), vice-presidents (assistant coaches), and upper management (captains/seniors) should not just be observers. They should share in the building process and humanize themselves to the hourly workers (who they may rarely see). I participated in a department wide team-building event where one of the exercises involved small group, jigsaw puzzle solving. The athletic director, who was also a vice-president, worked side by side with a department secretary, a twenty-two-year-old assistant coach, and a student athletic-trainer. In that case, new relationships were forged that probably would never have been without the team building activity.

Here are a few things to think about as you create the Useful Debate part of your culture: Are employee roles and job responsibilities clearly defined for everyone to see? Ultimately, the leader of a given project is the one who will often make the final decision. They may or may not take the suggestions offered, but it should be clear to everyone who has the final say on that venture's direction.

For projects that potentially have significant inherit conflict, these employee-to-employee discussions should not take place the way so many do—by email. There is too much room for inaccurate interpretation of the tone. Seeing facial expressions and hearing voice tone provides a much more accurate impression when it comes to deciphering meaning. This is a big reason why so many companies use telepresence video conferencing when it is not practical to meet in person. Unnecessary problems stagnate collaboration due to people having their feelings hurt or becoming angry over misunderstanding tone from text or email. Before the manager needs to get involved there should be an understanding in your workplace culture of how conversations should happen. Team conversations that may be fraught with heated differences of opinion should take place in-person or through video.

You cannot manage an adverse work relationship between employees or departments if you do not know it's happening. In college sports, many teams have a version of a Leadership Council. Typically these groups consist of the captains and at least one representative from each class (i.e. a freshman, sophomore, junior, and a senior). The councils I put together had two purposes: First, to educate this group of student-athletes on how to best lead. It's a subject for a completely different book, but most team captains are average at best when it comes to leadership. Predominantly because leading well is challenging and they have never been taught the skills to be a good leader. The second reason I met with my Leadership Council every other week was to find out if there were any negative team issues brewing below the surface. We would end each meeting with the corresponding class representative answering two questions: Was there anything the rest of the council could do to help them with any concerns relative to their class, be it academic, athletic, or personal? Second, were there concerns they had regarding their class and any conflict that needed to be arbitrated?

The first step of embracing the concept of conflict is to acknowledge and encourage it—with boundaries. Conflict is a necessary part of growth. But, there is a diminishing return on the value of conflict if it crosses the line and becomes a personal attack. The caveat to this is something most of us can relate to. There is a percentage of people who have such thin skin or are so insecure that any conflict is taken as a personal attack against them, from which they cannot recover without a visit to HR and a personal day off.

Relevant

A strong culture model means nothing if employees aren't made to feel **Relevant** by both management and their peers. If you skipped over the chapter titled "Matter", go back and read it now. Employees who feel relevant and valued are more committed, more engaged, and will produce significantly better results for the company than those who don't. Staff who feel they don't count and aren't relevant often leave.

Empower

Engagement and **Empowerment** go hand-in-hand. One of the key takeaways in an engagement study with almost 7,000 employees was that employees who felt a low level of empowerment were rated with engagement at the 24th percentile, versus highly empowered employees who were engaged at the 79th percentile. Even with some error or extraneous variables, the difference between these two numbers is astounding. Empowered employees are more loyal and more productive.

Keep in mind that entrusting authority to others can backfire if there isn't some structure to the process. A friend of mine recently called me to report on the disaster in progress relating to a new, young employee he had empowered. His exact words were, "We have created a monster." The employee's intentions were good, but they had begun regularly stepping outside the scope of their job and knowledge base trying to be helpful. In doing so they had caused multiple problems with customers by providing incorrect information. Upon further inspection, this employee had very little framework around what they could or could not do without approval. The "Go for it!" management approach was failing and with it came customer backlash and office discord.

The first question you need to ask yourself is: "Is this employee trained to be able to handle the authority and responsibility that comes with being empowered to make decisions autonomously?" If not, go no further until you train them how to handle the next tier of decision making in their job. The next step, prior to actually empowering them to make significant decisions, is to listen. You can give the initial gift of empowerment simply by having people feel heard. If their idea is something that makes sense you can act on it or allow them to run with this *one* idea. As they show signs of success with autonomous individual tasks, now is the time to open it up a bit more—with parameters. Where are the borders with regard to how much freedom they have to act autonomously? What areas are outside their purview? The story I told previously about "creating a monster" was due, in large part, to empowerment with no boundaries.

The second reason to empower your team members is that when there is a need for action or change that may prove unpopular, having empowered assistant managers or entrusted veteran employees will help bridge the buy-in gap between management and staff. The loyalty factor, due to prior empowerment, can help smooth the rocky road as your entrusted staff puts out fires you never see and helps ignite the employees' support of the new mission. Asking unempowered assistants or top employees to support you in a new directive can be like saying, "I know you don't feel I trust you or think you are responsible enough to make autonomous decisions, but I'd really appreciate it if you had my back with the potential staff blowback on the new program we are rolling out next week." This type of communication happens regularly in businesses. If employees feel valued and empowered, they are more likely to support the mission during trying times.

One spring we tested empowering our players to improve individual performance. Our staff identified the need for more individual skill development in order for us to advance as a team. We gave ownership to our players and decided to do this by empowering our student-athletes. The approach was to ask every player to find time each week to add two individually directed (no coach present) twenty-minute practice sessions. We explained that this was not going to be a short-term success, rather their work would pay off down the road. The twenty-minute sessions could be before practice, after practice, or on a day we did not have training scheduled. For any of you who may work for the NCAA, not to worry, we counted these sessions within our allowable weekly training time! We provided six areas where each player could direct their twenty-minute training. Each week the players logged their time in the corresponding skill development area. We put these into a color-coded spreadsheet so the team would be visually impacted by seeing twenty or so players commit to multiple sessions each week. At the end of the spring season we created a poster board that was astounding. There were hundreds of colored blocks displaying twenty-minute commitments. After implementing this for our spring season, we continued a version of the commitment through the following fall. Twelve months after starting our empowerment experiment we entered the next spring soccer season. It was the first spring season in the documented history of the soccer program that the team went undefeated. The product we put on the field that year was outstanding. I believe our success was a direct result of empowering our players to take personal responsibility over their evolution as individuals and as a team. Not to be lost in all of this is the compounding effect of single efforts which, combined with other efforts, equal a sum greater than their individual parts. Simplifying it, if you can have multiple employees improve their performance, in part due to being empowered, their combined results can create an unstoppable force.

Keep in mind, some people do not want to be empowered. Don't assume that every team member wants to be empowered and take on responsibility. I saw this regularly in sports. A junior or senior would be voted or appointed captain, only to be dreadful at carrying out the duties of the position. One tactic I employed was to request players who were interested in being considered for a leadership role to submit a paragraph or two as to why they would be a good fit for that position. This helped eliminate at least half of the problem—putting someone in a role where they have to make team-wide decisions and provide direction when they have no interest in said role.

(Safe)

I added the (S) at the end of CULTURE because **Safe** is often used when organizations are describing the idea of making their workplace an environment where employees can feel safe letting their superiors know what they dislike and what management needs to do better. In my opinion, *safe* is the most overused, erroneous component of many corporate culture statements. The concept of encouraging feedback is admirable and certainly can help a business grow that truly does employ this. But herein lies the problem. It goes against human nature to encourage criticism of oneself, especially considering the hierarchy of corporate structure. It would be uncommon for a manager to be genuinely open to critique from staff who have neither achieved the position in the company nor had the same amount of experience as the manager. The other side of the coin is the employee's willingness to potentially risk their job by openly judging a superior.

Here are some potential solutions. There are a plethora of anonymous 360 feedback tools worth considering. But employees are often concerned that their comments will still be tracked back to them. Remember building relationships earlier in the chapter? Relationships that spanned multiple hierarchal tiers? If you want a shot at receiving at least a snippet of criticism from a subordinate, build a trusting relationship with them. How you phrase the questions plays a big part in assuring that you receive an answer. Change, *"What can I do better?"* to *"What can we do better as a company?"* Then the answer will be a critique of the business, not necessarily of the individual. Where these conversations take place is also important. In a formal setting, with you behind your desk, the employee is less likely to speak freely than if you are in a more casual conversational atmosphere. If you are using a faceless tool for feedback, consider asking the employees to identify your top three to five strengths, from a list of ten. They are more likely to feel comfortable honestly identifying your strengths rather than your weaknesses. Combine multiple employee assessments and you can then recognize areas without any strength ratings. This information could tell you that some of those areas may be weaknesses. If your goal is to grow yourself and the company using as many resources as possible, you will need to be creative in how you procure feedback and be accepting of criticism.

It is easy to talk about great culture when things go well. The culture test comes when you have a bad season in sports or a poor quarter in the business world. There is a somewhat overused, but true phrase thrown around in athletics. The origins of this expression started with, "Adversity builds character." The next generation of the idiom became, "Adversity doesn't build character, it reveals it." This is absolutely true for culture. If you have a great culture, your team will survive and even thrive during periods of adversity and setbacks. During these times of difficulty, if your culture seems to wane more than it should, then it was probably built on erroneous pillars or it does not have a solid foundation. Erroneous pillars would be things on which you place high importance but are either insignificant to culture or are not tangible. They aren't easy for the employees to see, understand, and get behind. If the culprit is the lack of a solid foundation, that means your pillars may be good but your leadership group (president, CEO, managers) does not embody these core values on a daily basis. The employees understand the culture but do not actualize it because the management doesn't embody it. The people in charge talk the talk but don't walk the walk. Do not spend time drawing up a model of what you want the culture to be if you aren't willing to live it. Additionally, you need to be prepared to hold your team accountable to the culture you establish.

Expect disappointment and frustration during failures, it's human nature. But if the behaviors and attitudes that come in response to setbacks are negative, and opposite of your culture, then your culture was not what you thought it was. Culture can sustain teams during difficult times where others flounder. If it is any consolation, rarely do new coaches get culture right the first time out. There are learning curves as they appraise their team and there is some trial and error involved in creating a great culture where there wasn't one before.

You are now an arms dealer for culture. You have a blueprint with which to bring positive change. It is always the same place where new culture plans break down: failing to regularly maintain a commitment to uphold the standards. A friend of mine starts every weekly meeting with his leadership team with thirty minutes devoted to their message around culture. His team in turn disseminates this to their direct reports.

The culture standards should be visible to ensure that it is never far from employees' minds. Consider spending a few dollars printing large graphics with the words that embody your culture and placing them in visible spots around your building. Make a commitment to regularly making culture part of the daily heartbeat that is your organization.

PART 2

EMPLOYEE REVIEWS

The second part of the book covers important engagement pitfalls outside of the $E=MC^4$ formula and the corresponding solutions. We will start with the employee review. One of the surest ways to unleash a wave of dread and create a potential disengagement opportunity in your company is to stick to the old school model of annual employee performance reviews as your main assessment and motivation tool. In a People IQ survey, 87% of managers and employees felt annual reviews were ineffective and not useful. There are dozens of polls out there that all confirm the same. The way many of these meetings are run, it could be mistaken for a Parent-Teacher-Student conference in grade school. *Now Johnny, you need to play nicer on the playground or you will lose recess time, okay? Do you promise to behave better in Ms. Johnson's class and turn your homework in on time? Be a good boy Johnny and run along now.* Because teachers (and coaches) almost always provide immediate feedback—not waiting until the end of the year to applaud or correct behavior—none of this is a new revelation for Johnny. His parents, on the other hand, are concerned, bewildered, and have plenty of questions. The takeaway from this is not to send your parents to your annual review—although that has actually been attempted in today's helicopter parenting world—it is to revamp these archaic forums that are often just a "check the box" for managers. *I had my annual meeting with my employee.* Check. *I told them what they need to do better.* Check. *Through a veiled conversation I kind of let them know if their performance doesn't improve they may be terminated. I am fairly certain my staff member left the review disheartened and demoralized.* Check. The model is flawed; let's fix it.

I believe the real purpose—and not a good one—of traditional annual performance reviews is twofold. For managers who are not good at coaching employees, and are poor communicators, it's their opportunity to formally have a one-way conversation about standards that are not being met. Second, they take place to put an employee on notice so that if they were to be fired, there is a Human Resources paper trail documenting the situation. If you operate a business where it is difficult to terminate someone without thorough documentation, these assessments may lessen the likelihood of a wrongful termination lawsuit.

The performance review was put on this planet for primarily one reason: to assess an employee's ACCOUNTABILITY. Specifically, their accountability as it pertains to performance. There are numerous formats with which to accomplish this. The outdated traditional model can achieve it, but with an awful aftertaste and some negative side effects. We are after a version that is the Holy Grail. We want an accountability process that also improves engagement, performance, morale, and profitability. You simply cannot check all of these boxes with the time-honored review in its current state.

Let's start with the desired end results in mind. We identified those in the prior paragraph. Before we even begin thinking about a review process, we want the goals to be things along those lines: accountable, happy, hard-working, productive team members who feel heard, enjoy where they work, and are great ambassadors for the company. These goals will help the business thrive while driving recruitment and retention. We want to minimize any actions that will negatively impact those. A review process which over 80% of the employees and managers don't think is valuable would be a negative impactor. A system where the initial feelings going in are worry and nausea, does not align with the goals above. Do you really want to continue a practice where relief is universally accepted as a great conclusion to the meeting? It is time for a change.

But I use the compliment sandwich method during our reviews to let staff know what they are doing well and what they need to improve. In the formal review setting, employees are on the edge of their seats waiting for the real or perceived threat to be delivered. Your compliment sandwich can have Kobe Wagyu beef (at up to $300 per pound), a delightfully pungent White Stilton cheese, a thin layer of Beluga caviar and the best artesian bread flown in from Paris. But the employee knows that there is a yet unmentioned layer to their sandwich. That's what they are anticipating and where their focus is. The blanket of sardines (my apologies to those brave souls who ingest these willingly) is hidden below the cheese and will overpower all the other layers. You have a very expensive sandwich that is just going to leave an offensive taste in someone's mouth. The compliment sandwich needs to be taken off the menu.

To get the most out of your team, build them up. Constructive criticism is of course necessary, but formally delivering it from a fire hose once a year does little to build people up. Most employees head into these reviews having some degree of apprehension, bordering on fear. If you are performing your job as a manager, your employees know (in real time) what they are doing well and what they need to improve. Build casual check-ins into opportunities to have conversations about what the employee is contributing positively as well as areas for improvement. These can take place weekly or monthly. Make it a point to find time to review what is going well and what has room for development. Just avoid having all of these occur in a formal setting and as a scheduled meeting. If you have a standing monthly meeting in your office with each employee, that's great, but you should find time to accomplish the same thing during the other three weeks of the month in a less intimidating setting. Stop by their office. Take a walk down the hall with them. Join them in the break room for a cup of coffee. Choose a particular project, sale, or meeting they have had or are preparing for and have them direct the conversation to answer: (1)What went well? (2)Where is there room for improvement? (3)What can you do to help them? You have just conducted a micro-review in five minutes with an opportunity to provide immediate feedback from your end.

There are multiple areas in which an employee is assessed. Strategically take an element of the job during each check-in to integrate a **two-way** conversation about that area of performance. Every one of your check-in chats should have you asking your employee, *What can I do to help you be successful?*

As a head coach, I only recall two times in my career ever being asked by my direct report or athletic director during a review, *What can we do to help you and your program be successful?* I certainly received my share of implied job threats about what I needed to do better (always to win more games). On the contrary, I tried to end every player meeting I had with, *What can we do for you?*

Many businesses and universities alike use a numeric scale to conduct their reviews. One of the universities I worked for had a 1 to 3 scale, another used a 1 to 5 scale. They can be a good way to measure improvements from year to year but they are usually so subjective that their accuracy and significance is negligible. There can also be unintended disengagement as a result of assigning a number to an individual. There are successful, motivated, and committed employees who may receive a 3.8 average on a 1-5 scale (5 being very good). The manager thinks of this as a complimentary grade. The employee may leave the review completely demoralized.

For the 1 to 3 scale, 1 equaled unsatisfactory, 2 was satisfactory, and 3 was good. Most of the coaches and staff who shared their results with me regularly received 2's. Think about that for a minute. You spend twelve months passionately committed to your job (as most are in college athletics), working 50 to 80 hours a week, only to come out of your meeting with a pat on the back and a "satisfactory" performance award, based primarily on one supervisor's assessment of you. The school that I worked for with the 1 to 3 scale had a very public, but unwritten axiom: *Don't give out 3s because then the employee has no room or motivation to grow.* I witnessed some incredible coaching performances receive 2s due to this primitive and unsound reasoning. If someone earns a 3, give them a 3! How these scales and reviews are still employed by leadership who supposedly have remarkable acumen in higher education is beyond me. I would venture to guess that the people behind the implementation of many of these reviews don't actually go through the same review process themselves. If they did the process would undoubtedly change.

Whether the review takes the shape of the antiquated traditional style or something more modern, such as regular check-ins, the pillars of your company's culture must be included. It is fundamental that employee behavior is appraised relative to the culture standard as well as the evaluation being based on goals and performance. Previously you read about making sure mission, vision, and culture were easily understood by everyone from the CEO to the hourly employees. There is no better time to ensure that this is true than when members of your team are completing a self-evaluation or being evaluated by a supervisor. A glaring example of how ambiguous standards can cause problems during evaluation time comes from one of the evaluations administered at a university where I worked. One area we had to self-rate, as well as being ranked by our superior, was called *Magis*. A Latin adverb, it means *more,* or maybe it means *excellence,* or some say *generosity*. There are no less than a dozen interpretations of the word. We actually had a staff meeting and the word was its own agenda item. Okay, well it would have been if agendas were distributed. Maybe we would finally get some clarity on Magis and how to rate it. What happened next was akin to a 7-year-old trying to describe quantum physics to a class of other 7-year-olds. We left the meeting more confused about this area of the evaluation. The positive part of Magis on the assessment was that since absolutely no one understood it, including management, how could you be wrong if you gave yourself a perfect 3?

On average, 1% of U.S. employees are terminated each year. For many of the 99% who will not lose their jobs, all the primitive evaluation does is demoralize and demotivate them. To be clear, I am not saying that criticism doesn't have a place in reviews or check-ins. When you need to be critical, let them see the implications of what could happen negatively or positively for the business based on their actions. If there are significant problems and the employee is in jeopardy of being terminated, by all means they deserve this information.

Back to athletics. Due to recruiting and games, college coaches work well beyond the traditional 40-hour work week. They go months at a time without a day off. Non-coaching athletic department staff often get home at 10:00 or 11:00 p.m. due to covering university sporting events. When coaches and staff came out of their reviews with even a three ranking (out of 3) it was simply a relief to be done with it. There were usually very few motivating or helpful takeaways coming out of these meetings. If a coach had a good year, their excitement was tempered rather quickly during the annual review when it became clear that by being successful, they had just raised the expectation bar and needed to meet it the following season. The implied, "*or else*" was always floating out there. The same goes for many corporate America employees. An employee had a great year and crushed their sales goals. Typically, a new performance standard is then set by management for the following year. If burning out your staff and compromising their quality of life is the goal, then by all means, employ this method. Just be upfront in the hiring process that this is how the business operates. Some people do work just fine in this environment. The secret to how an employer rewards a team member for great performance, but also lets them know that they have upped the ante in terms of expected targets, lies in goal setting (coming in the next chapter). If your company truly values linking the bottom line—outstanding employee performance—with earnest consideration of balancing the destructive duress that comes with the elusive ever-changing corporate goals target, consider revamping your review process.

All of this potential productive development will of course be demolished if your check-ins or meetings feel like micromanagement to the employee. It's not how **you** feel about your managing and meeting, it is how your team member feels. If they sense they are being micromanaged during these sessions the value of your newfound approach will be diminished significantly. While daily check-ins can be too much in terms of a perceived lack of empowerment by the employee, you should have daily face-time with each person under you. If you do not, either the reporting structure needs to be changed or you should reevaluate how often you are getting out of your office and making the rounds. A "daily face to face" is NOT a meeting, it's a conversation and does not need to have anything to do with the business. Remember from the Connect chapter, building relationships happens in personal, non-structured moments that are not about work.

If your employees—not you—feel the reviews add value to the individual, the team, the division, and the company, you are doing something right with your system. Keep looking to fine-tune it based on employee feedback and industrial and organizational psychology research.

For the traditionalists who think I've gone soft and feel employees need to be coddled, that would be incorrect. What is the purpose of your annual review? To provide feedback about job performance. To promote communication. To provide data which can be used to determine a promotion or firing. Let's break those down individually. (1) Feedback: Once a year you are going to give feedback. You are too late. The patterns and behaviors you want to correct have gone unchecked for months. The lost revenue cannot be recouped. You should have been having informal check-ins every two weeks or so. (2) Communication: Hoping to promote good communication by meeting formally once a year is absurd. Good communication is built during regular, informal moments. (3) Data: Historical data of an employee's performance can certainly be used to make career path determinations, but can't you make the same decisions about an employee without arbitrarily putting a number or a grade on them in a meeting once a year? Companies do have an understandable litigious concern over not promoting employees equally, thus if they have a grade they can justify their decisions easier. Depending on your business structure you may still need to have a rating but that can be done within a more productive setting than the yearly meeting.

My reviews were always conducted very professionally, but at the same time many of those had undertones of job threats. Coaches are one of the groups who "get it." You don't need to regularly explain to a coach that losing will eventually cost them their job. In the medical field, good physicians need to let their patient know of a terminal diagnosis. Those physicians don't continue to meet with the patient just to reiterate to them that they may die if the doctors cannot turn things around. They try to figure out what else they can do to help the patient. They problem solve. If you do annual performance reviews, are you trying to problem solve for underperforming employees or are you just checking the boxes HR needs when it comes time to terminate? I understand that some form of these annual reviews are necessary. Fortunately, many businesses are starting to recognize the complete lack of value these reviews have in their traditional form. If Dell, Microsoft, Goldman Sachs, and IBM can break the mold of the old school review, maybe you can too.

GOAL SETTING

If you have read my book *Cope, Rise, Thrive!* many of the following goal setting strategies will sound familiar. Goals, specifically high goals, are woven into the fabric of every successful sports team. According to research out of the University of Scranton, 92% of people fail to achieve their goals. In my experience, this is due in large part to the widely accepted, but ineffective model of goal setting. There is very little that is motivational about the classic model. Traditional goal setting often ends once the goal is set. No wonder there is such a high percent of failure. Personally, I'm rarely as inspired by just writing down a goal as I am when I do it through a vision board combined with an easy to follow method. Oftentimes, after writing down a goal, people are at a loss when it comes to their next step. Committing to reevaluating and sustaining the process while maintaining any sense of enthusiasm is a huge challenge with traditional goal setting. Teams and businesses across the world eagerly commence this age-old ritual of SMART goal setting as a new year begins. For a refresher: S(Specific) M(Measurable) A(Achievable) R(Relevant) T(Time-bound). There is a better way! That said, time-honored SMART goal setting has some fine underlying principles which can be infused into a more workable, less paralyzing approach.

I have always encouraged people to consider setting two types of goals: *standard* goals and *stretch* goals. What I call standard goals are goals you feel you can attain, albeit with some work. Stretch goals are those that one would definitely consider substantial and very challenging to obtain. Don't be afraid of stretch goals. They can help drive you to otherwise elusive achievements.

Words on paper are enough to guide and motivate some people. Words are far more inspiring if they are tied to something more visual than just the font they are written in. I have a unique method which combines some principles of traditional goal setting with a more sustainable model of actually achieving those goals. It starts with a vision board (VB). If you are not familiar with one of these game-changers, Google "vision board images" then come back and join us. A classic VB will have pictures, words, and phrases all representing what you want to be, want to achieve, or want to have. It represents your goals and your dreams. A VB will help you maintain focus on your ambitions while providing motivation in that direction. If you are new to the vision board game and are now overwhelmed with the complex images of boards you found during your search, let's start with a simpler version. Let me tell you a story.

My father was a general aviation pilot. I can still recall the last flight I made with him. He rented a small plane with an instructor and off we went over the Blue Ridge

Mountains of Maryland. I was seven at the time and knew then that I wanted to fly. Seventeen, the age at which one can obtain his pilot's license, came and went with visions of flying still just a dream. At twenty-six, I became one of the youngest D1 collegiate head coaches in the country. Having a full-time job and control over my schedule, I thought this might be a good time to start flight training. Nope. Two years later I had moved up the coaching ranks and was living in Indianapolis, home to multiple small airports with flight schools. Each air show I went to renewed my desire to take flight, yet I remained grounded. Then, I experienced my first unintentional encounter with the beginnings of a vision board. I was an assistant at Indiana University and printed out a photo of an airplane which was for sale at the Bloomington Airport. The picture was pinned to my desk at eye level and I saw it every day. About a month later, I picked up the office phone and called BMG Aviation, at the airport. I asked if they provided flight instruction and the rest is history. On March 11, 2008, I had my introductory flight. One hundred fifty-two landings and ninety-five days later, I earned my PPL (Private Pilot License). A year after that, I had my Instrument Rating; one of the biggest accomplishments in my life. About thirty years had gone by from when I first thought about becoming a pilot. Nothing happened during that window to cause me to take action toward that goal until I put the photo up on my desk. That serendipitous moment was the only thing I did differently during those three decades in which visions of airplanes had danced in my head. The point being, you can start your vision board with just one photo and maybe a phrase or a word.

We will look at two versions of using a vision board: an individual and a business version. *Why do I care if my employees create their own personalized vision boards?* Because helping them build motivation and triumph in their personal lives will carry over to their work lives. Also, most likely their vision board will end up including something work related, like a promotion. An employee who is striving for a promotion is likely going to be more dedicated and driven, thus creating more success for the company. Self-serving for your business? Maybe. But it is a win-win for both sides.

Individually, it could be a new hobby someone wants to set a goal toward, or perhaps they want to put themselves in a financial position to purchase a second home. Maybe it is to become president of the regional bank they work for. They should choose an image and words that inspire them to direct action toward achieving that goal. I think we can all agree that a picture of a stunning 10,000 square foot house perched high on a hillside overlooking the Pacific Ocean at sunset is far more inspiring than just writing the goal, *"Own a second home."*

If you are making a board for your corporation, maybe a goal is a mocked-up cover of your city's business journal or quarterly newsletter that has your company listed as one of the "Top 5 Places to Work."

The stretch goal version of this would be to mock up a Time magazine cover with your business making the same list, but nationally. If that's too hackneyed for you, then put your own twist on it. For example, let's say top-notch customer service is a pillar and a goal. You could set a goal of winning an award presented by The American Business Awards in their Customer Service category. The picture on your VB would be the ABA logo or a photo of the award. A different idea for representing customer service on your board would be to set a positive customer feedback metric as your goal. Every customer has the opportunity to answer a one-question customer satisfaction survey. Maybe your goal is to have 90% of the surveys come back either at "very satisfied" or higher and that goal goes on your board. The process of taking the steps to build a VB will allow you to hone in on what is truly important to your company. It will galvanize your team to peel back the onion and establish what is of critical importance.

Now, pick a couple of goals that are all going to go on the same board. Mentally split your vision board vertically down the middle. There is no need to draw an actual line, but you can. You now have a left and a right side to the VB. Start with the right side. These are the Outcome Goals. The new hobby, the vacation house, or work promotion. Or, for the corporate VB, the Outcome Goals might be the customer satisfaction goal, a sales target, or the Best Places to Work goal. Insert images which represent these outcomes on the right side of your vision board. You may also have some energizing words of achievement or encouragement pasted on this side. Words or phrases you envision hearing from friends, family members, co-workers, or industry colleagues once you have accomplished one of these goals. For individuals, their vision board should be printed and put where they can see it daily. For companies, the VB should be blown up and put in prominent places around the office, possibly even as a screen saver on everyone's computers.

On the left side of the board will be your **Process Goals**. These are the things you need to do every day or every week in order to achieve your **Outcome Goals**. On my board, I have an image that says, "Take Action Everyday." There is a red "action" button in this image. This is my reminder that every day I need to do at least one thing that will contribute to one of my Outcome Goals. It could be sending an email soliciting a speaking engagement or working on my next book. I don't go a day without taking at least one action, and usually far more, toward an Outcome Goal. I have a photo of a flower growing up through asphalt. This is my reminder that I will get "paved over" or rejected, and I must be resilient. There was an image on the Process side of my VB with multiple radio and TV stations. For me to grow my business and reach my Outcome Goals, this was my goal of connecting with media outlets trying to secure a booking to promote my program on TV or radio. I added this image to my VB in July. Now we come to the idea that goals must have a timeline assigned to them. The difference between a goal and a dream: <u>Action and a Timeline</u>. Dreams are open ended, goals are not. Concealed in my TV/radio image goal was a timeline. It was hidden in the form of a radio station. I inserted "101.8" into the image amongst the other TV and radio images. This appeared to be a radio station but was actually my goal timeline of $^{10}/_{18}$ or October 31, 2018. This was the date I had given myself to have participated in an interview on TV or radio. On October 27, 2018, four days before my deadline, I did an interview on Fox TV. Be creative with your Goal Setting Vision Board! Would I have achieved that goal without a timeline? We will never know, but I believe having that timeline compelled it to happen.

Here is where everyone gets caught up in any version of goal setting: failure. Your timeline comes, and you have or have not met your goal. You received the promotion or you did not. Your company reduced business expenses by the lofty 20% goal or did not. You increased your website traffic by 15% or you did not. You reached your sales goal or did not. For the select few who achieve the high goals they set, all is well in the world. But most people will not reach all of their goals, especially if they are set high enough from the start. If you regularly reach all of your goals, you need to raise the bar and expand your vision. You are capable of much more. For the large majority of those who don't reach all their goals, the response is to perceive it as failure, and that's the end of goal setting for them. We need to reframe what goal setting success looks like.

Visualize a 1 to 10 scale running horizontally from left to right across the middle of your vision board. Every half inch or so is the next number. The number 1 should be on the far left and the number 10 is just inside the right hand border of the paper. Instead of classifying each goal as either achieved or failed, think of assigning a 1 to 10 to every goal once the deadline comes. Let's look at the goal of trying to cut expenses by 20%, which we set as a lofty or stretch goal. For arguments sake we only cut costs by 15%. In traditional goal setting, this particular one gets interred in the graveyard of failure. We are left to ponder how morale will be when we share this setback with our team. All that work only to fail. Or did we? On our number scale, a 10 would have been assigned had we had exceeded 20% cuts. A 9 would have been attained if we hit our target number. Cutting expenses by 15% puts us at about a 7 on the scale. If we had not set the stretch goal of 20%, would we have put in the amount of strategic planning and work required to cut even 15%? Probably not. While 15% did not meet the percent we aspired to, it can and should be looked at as successful.

For our corporate example, if you only cut costs by a couple percentage points, while one could argue that is some degree of success, either your target was way off or the process goals were unsound, not followed, or out of sequence. Additionally, ask yourself, "Did I provide my team the necessary resources to achieve this goal?" As you delve into goal setting and explore the process outside of its traditional boundaries, you will find value beyond what you have imagined. If you are cemented in conventional goal setting where everything is either achieved or failed, you will be missing a tremendous amount of "partial triumph" achievement. Achievement you can build upon.

For your Big Vision or Stretch Goals, keep these two words at the forefront: Momentum and Sequencing. (For the visual that follows in this paragraph, you may need to read it twice to fully understand it.) Picture a row of ten dominos, standing on their ends. Each domino is its own goal. Imagine each domino is twice the size of the one prior to it. The first domino is two inches tall, the second is four inches tall and the tenth is eighty-five feet high, the height of an eight-story building. The tenth is our Big Vision or Stretch Goal domino. If you were to tip the first domino over, it would knock the second down. As the second falls, it will drop the third, and so forth until the final domino collapses under the force of the ninth. Now let's change the order of the dominos as we set them up. We will put the sixth domino, which is about five feet tall, in the third spot. The first domino falls into the second; the second, which is four inches high, falls into our new domino in the third position, and it doesn't move. We are stopped, eight dominos short of our stretch goal. Not even close to knocking it down. Where did we go wrong? Obviously at the third domino. It was out of <u>sequence</u>. It was far too large to be knocked over by the much smaller and lighter second domino. As you set and check off your weekly process goals, make sure the sequencing is right. You start with small achievable goals which lead you down the path of ultimately reaching the end goal. Think big, but start small. Each goal will progressively give you more and more confidence towards your dream goal. By just achieving some small goals at the beginning you are building an unstoppable force: momentum.

As you begin to experience success in goal setting, be wary of the trap that lies ahead. Many who find success end up growing complacent with the achievement they experience. They don't take the opportunity to build upon it. A small group embrace the successful process, feed off it, and double down their goal setting efforts for the future. But most wallow in their accomplishments and forget what got them there. They begin to believe the hype around themselves or their company.

A final word on goal setting and one of the biggest differences between how it is often carried out in the sports world versus the corporate framework: The athletes are almost always directly involved in the setting of individual and team goals. They are a significant part of the conversation and their thoughts are resolutely considered. This is not always the case in business settings. Employees are often given their goals at the beginning of each year and the team goals are established with little to no say from the actual people who will be responsible for making sure these goals are met. You have a far greater chance of meeting a goal if there is buy-in and ownership. Follow through will be greater if the emergence of these goals is directly linked to the people charged with meeting them.

GOAL SETTING SQUARE

Now that you have the basics of VB Goal Setting it's time to take goal setting to the next level by combining the visual piece of it with the practical part of it. You will build one Square for each of your goals. Once your Squares are completed, I would encourage you to hang them next to your VB. Just as there were individual employee vision boards and corporate-wide vision boards, the same goes for the goal setting Square. The following example is for a specific individual. As mentioned previously you can build Squares for company-wide goals as well. The reason I am going to build out a Square for an employee and not a large-scale corporate goal is this: You can set all of the grand business goals you want, but ultimately the success of these goals will be determined by individuals and their ability to set and achieve specific objectives. Also, don't underestimate the value of helping employees set and build their own personal goals. Individual growth and development—which takes place with goal setting—directly correlates with employee engagement. Help them with advancement and promotion opportunities, most likely you will receive a return on your investment in the form of increased productivity and improved levels of engagement.

You start by working backwards. I am going to show you (see actual Square below) how to reverse engineer goal setting. You can build a Square based around any timeline you choose. It could be a goal that will take three months or five years to achieve. Give some thought to the timeline. Maybe it's more like a ten-year goal.

The goal is to become an Executive Director in two years. If you are early in your career when you identify this goal, then possibly it's five years in the making. The first objective completed in the blank Square will be your outcome goal—*Executive Director*—written in the bottom right corner. Next, move on to the "1 Year" portion of the square. It is what you need to have accomplished a year from today. To be on track for ED, you will probably have to exceed your sales goals, and find leadership opportunities. These are two key components which employees chasing an ED position need to have in order to distinguish themselves.

For the three-month portion you will need to complete a strengths and weaknesses assessment of your current sales skills and connect with three EDs in your company. Your S&W assessment can come from objectively identifying these (hard to do for some), as well as soliciting opinions of your strengths and weaknesses from superiors and co-workers. There are also online tools to work with, including anonymous surveys submitted by your clients and co-workers. If you are using a client it should be one with whom you have had a relationship for a while. Also, you are not conducting a "satisfaction survey." That is something different. You are being up front that you are trying to identify strengths and weaknesses and will appreciate their honesty. Knowing your deficiencies and assets is directly linked with your ability to increase sales.

The reason you are connecting with three EDs is multi-faceted. These EDs obviously did something right to get where they are. You are trying to pick up on the critical behaviors to emulate, to identify the knowledge base for the position, to pinpoint potential pitfalls, and to help yourself navigate through the organization. Additionally, EDs are leaders and can help you with the process of finding leadership opportunities. By building relationships with EDs you will foster key people who can champion your own rise.

One month in, the goal is to have completed research on the various tools available for conducting a strength and weakness assessment and to have identified from whom to solicit feedback. Additionally, you should have a short list completed of potential EDs to connect with.

The weekly goal appears as a sticky note in the center of the Square which can be changed out as needed. Week 1 goal: Schedule a meeting with senior management and clearly document the agenda for the meeting. This will force you to put your goals out there which is the first step toward realizing success.

If the main four boxes in the Square are the WHAT, the weekly goals is the HOW. For our corporate individual, let's look at the three-month portion: Strengths and Weaknesses/Connected with Three EDs. To reach those in three months you will need to start doing some research into tools which help you identify S&W—particularly those that will hurt or help your ability to make sales. You will begin working on a list of associates, friends, and family members who may be willing to help you identify these. Second, come up with a list of the current EDs in your building, region, state, etc. Look into their corporate profile to see if there are any shared backgrounds the two of you have. Finding some common ground would allow for an easier introduction if you have never met them. Maybe you attended the same college or lived in the same city at some point. They could have children the same age as yours. These steps can play out on weekly sticky notes.

For example, week one, after your meeting with management, your goal is to create a list of ten EDs in your company who might be potential ED mentor prospects. Week two you will start on your S&W goal, researching some online tools and articles helping with S&W assessment. Week three you are back to the ED goal, breaking down that list into profiles of some who appear to be the most approachable. This could be based on their location. They may work in your building or in the same city in a different location so the chances of you running into them are greater. It could be due to you hearing a lot of positives about a particular ED. This is where you do some investigating into their backgrounds to see if you share anything in common. Week four it's back to S&W. You have learned some different approaches to S&W assessment and you are going to put together your list of people to whom you will be reaching out for feedback. Week five, your goal is to connect and secure an introductory meeting with them. At the end of three months you should now have completed your S&W assessment and built initial relationships with three EDs. You don't have to alternate weeks between S&W and connecting with EDs. It's just one way to break down your weekly goals. Don't be overwhelmed with the process. It can seem like a lot, each week devoting additional time working on the weekly goal. It's really not. We are talking fifteen to twenty minutes a day. Goal setting, and more importantly achieving those goals, is less about an exact weekly science than it is about regularly taking some positive action towards accomplishing your goals.

The same Square design could be used to set any goal. Maybe it's Increasing Website Sales by x%, Decreasing Overhead Expenses by x%, Reducing Employee Turnover by x%, etc. Improving behaviors is ultimately what gives you or your business more successful outcomes. Properly setting goals will allow you to focus on targets and implement a plan that, at its core, will drive sustainable behavior change, change that will move mountains.

LEADERSHIP COUNCIL

Remember the Leadership Council used in athletics where a member of each class—freshmen through senior—is chosen to join the captains and form a group that meets with the coaches weekly or bi-weekly? Does your business have one? Most likely you do, kind of, in the form of C-suite executives who meet regularly. Great start. Now consider adopting a model closer to what we see among sports teams. The big difference— most corporate versions of leadership teams do not have "freshmen" or "sophomores" as members. They wouldn't dare bring someone in who is so inexperienced in terms of understanding management and who is far from qualified to weigh in on important company policies and decisions. Or are they?

On a corporate Leadership Council the *coaches* are the CEO, CFO, President and a few other "C" designated employees. The *team captains* are upper management. *Juniors* and *Seniors* are assistant managers, *sophomores* are tenured respected staff and *freshmen* are the every-day folks who make up the majority of your workforce. *But we don't need a council. We have some of the brightest and best on our executive management team.* As Don Myer, one of the winningest college basketball coaches of all time would ask, *Who's running your locker room?* What is happening in the "locker rooms" throughout your corporate campus? Surely your CEO or president cannot be at every water cooler, in every break room, and sitting at each cubicle complex throughout the organization. But members of your council can be. Members who can do two things in those venues: First, have their thumb on the pulse of the organization. They will hear what's going well, what the concerns are, and sense the corporate heartbeat. They are more in touch than the C-suite folks are with the workforce. Second, the council should be able to better understand and thus support the company message. Possibly a new initiative is being rolled out and it will inevitably receive some push back. It is vital that the concerns be identified immediately before they can take the form of a snowball, gaining size and momentum, ultimately crushing the new concept. Executive leadership will likely not be the first to hear about opposition. It will be those with boots on the ground, your first line of defense. The ones whose voices can combat the inescapable embers that are certain to smolder and ignite a blaze if not extinguished early.

In the collegiate athletics setting, council members are often solely voted onto the council by their teammates. This sometimes takes the form of what appears to be a "popularity contest." While it is important to make sure your selections do have at least partial support of their peers, the choices must be filtered by company leadership. Peer nominations should be looked at as "suggestions." Ultimately, the council members must be able to live the core values and culture on a daily basis at an elite level. You will sabotage yourself if you select members who do not or cannot model the expected standards.

Building the locker room leadership model out further, let's turn to a quote by famed Duke basketball coach, Mike Krzyzewski: "The single most important ingredient after you get the talent is internal leadership. It's not the coaches as much as one single person or a few people on the team who set higher standards than the team would normally set itself." The late Skip Prosser, the only coach in NCAA basketball history to take three separate schools to the NCAA tournament his first year coaching the teams, told me something similar years ago. He said, "It's what happens when the coaches walk out of the locker room that makes good teams great. We can only do so much as coaches. At some point, it's up to the players to control the destiny. The voices in the locker room is where that happens." Having the right people embedded in your leadership council allow standards to be modeled and scaled out at a level that coaches, or upper management, simply cannot reach.

The additional team members who make up the council do not need to be part of the weekly upper management meeting, but they should be brought in monthly, quarterly, or as needed. You don't want "as needed" to only be when there is a problem. These members must feel valued for their proactive contribution, not just reactively to help solve an unexpected issue. This could take place as part of the standing weekly upper management meeting or it might be its own separate forum. Some rules of order should be established from the beginning when you assemble the full council.

1. These are not gripe sessions.

2. If you offer up an obstacle or problem you should have the initial stages of a possible solution in mind.

3. It's not personal if your idea ultimately isn't adopted by executive leadership.

4. The "freshmen" and "sophomores" on the team need to know they are there to provide the pulse, they are NOT being asked to be "informants."

5. The front-line committee members must be trained on how to handle being "put in the middle" between management and the rest of the company.

6. TRUST between levels will make or break the effectiveness of the council.

7. See # 6.

STRENGTHS & WEAKNESSES

I am a non-traditionalist when it comes to my approach to strengths and weaknesses. I'll use a regularly occurring example from my coaching career to demonstrate this. One of the questions I would ask high school student-athletes we were recruiting was, "What part of your game do you feel, or do your coaches feel, you need to improve in order to be successful at the NCAA Division 1 level?" Inevitably, this question would produce one of the most communicative moments in our conversation. Since I coached soccer, the answer would go something like this: "My high school coach says I probably need to get a little better with my left foot, my heading needs to improve, my shooting is okay but I need more power, I need to develop a couple of really good moves to beat my defender and I must get stronger." If this young student-athlete were to actually commit to improving all of these, they would become average in all areas. They would not have the time needed to take all these parts of their game to an exceptional level. Meanwhile, the strengths they have will be neglected while they put their time into improving shortcomings. The focus often seems to be on the weaknesses while it should be on the strengths.

This is my approach for you to excel at a high level, no matter what you do. Identify any significant weaknesses that will prevent you from achieving your goal. If you want to be an accountant and are not good at math, this would be a significant weakness which would need to be addressed. Another thought as you approach weaknesses: do you need to improve a particular weakness or can you just work around it? Next, identify something that is already a strength and put together a plan to make it a world-class strength. Become the best in this one area among all your peers or co-workers. I can give countless examples of players who went on to great college careers because they had one strength that was dominant and we needed them on the field for it. Other areas of their game may have been very average, but there was one thing they did better than anyone else and that's what made them so valuable. Again, if you have a glaring weakness which will definitely inhibit your chances of success in a given endeavor, you do need to address this particular weakness. Just don't forget to take your strength, water it, feed it, nurture it, and continue to build it to a level which separates you from your peers.

Take an area of your life, social, health, business, family, etc. Create two columns. List any weaknesses in that particular area of your life on the left side. Circle the ones that are so weak they could limit your ability to succeed. Maybe you are working on your "family" list and recognize that your acute lack of patience is damaging your relationship with one of your children.

This could be a weakness that needs to be addressed. In the next column, write down your strengths. Circle one or two you are really good at and have chosen to make world class. Solicit feedback from close friends, your spouse and children if you like. Often, these folks will be apprehensive about giving you negative feedback but will most likely give you honest observations about your strengths. Break down each of the sections of your life this way. The second opportunity for you to constructively use this list is during difficult challenges. Knowing and focusing on your strengths when taking on something which causes you anxiety and uncertainty is a proven tactic. You have a presentation you will be delivering at a conference. It is a potentially intimidating environment. Your boss will be there. Possible future clients will attend. As you prepare your talk and the angst starts slithering in, remind yourself of those special strengths you have. This will help in a few ways. One, it will have the effect of pumping the brakes on a negative thought cycle that is starting to develop. Your focus will naturally switch to a more positive mindset. Second, it will feed your self-belief. Other than needing to know the material you are speaking on, self-belief is the most significant factor in your successful presentation.

Your angst about presenting at work or meeting with a crucial client will be minimized as you develop confidence. Confidence which comes from improving strengths and minimizing, or working around, key weaknesses. For many of the emotionally brittle athletes I coached, confidence, or a lack thereof, would make or break their athletic careers. Confidence exists both on the conscious and subconscious levels. The best way to build it is for your brain to have experienced repeated success over and over. If you want confidence at the free throw line as a basketball player, but haven't practiced hundreds of free throws, it may be hard to be confident.

Identifying individual employee strengths and helping them build on those is key. On a more scalable level, determine the one or two things your organization as a whole is going to be able to do exceptionally and commit to its development. Bottom line, your business is probably not going to be extraordinary unless you are able to do at least one thing at an outstanding level. While converting a weakness into an exceptional strength is possible, your time will be better spent fueling the fire of a strength which will ultimately separate you from the ordinary.

MEETINGS

I have a coffee mug that reads, "I survived another meeting that could have been accomplished with an email." The Harvard Business Review conducted a study with two-hundred executives and reported that only 17% of them felt their meetings were productive and a good use of time. A University of North Carolina study concluded that how workers feel about the effectiveness of meetings correlates with their job satisfaction—or more often—job dissatisfaction.

One terrific way to create employee disengagement is to have staff meetings just to have staff meetings. If you cannot define the agenda and purpose of the meeting ahead of time, put an embargo on it before it ever happens. By conducting the meeting you will lose credibility and frustrate employees who probably have actual work to do.

If you are leading the meeting and have a 'C' in your title, i.e. are in a powerful position, be aware of something that world-renowned business educator Marshall Goldsmith talks about—the plus 5%, minus 50% problem. It has to do with very smart people trying to add too much value in the form of opinions to every discussion topic. For example, employees propose new ideas and the boss leading the meeting consistently tries to "add value" to the ideas being generated around the table by adding suggestions to it. On the surface, nothing appears to be wrong with this idea, but Goldsmith says that the value added may be 5%, but the employee's commitment to execute the new idea may drop up to 50% because the idea is no longer solely theirs. You are potentially contributing to disengagement unintentionally. This is not to say there shouldn't be discussion and "useful debate," there should be. Just be careful that the additional conversation around the employee's idea isn't regularly coming from the person in a high-power position running the meeting. Again, I say be aware of this possibility, but obviously you cannot let it restrict your input when you feel the value add for the business with your tweaking is necessary. I look at this concept as more of an awareness not to continually interject "value adds" during the entire meeting if you do hold a position of power within the business.

As most college coaches will attest, athletic administrators like to have a lot of meetings, while coaches rarely organize a staff or team meeting unless it is essential. That doesn't mean the coaches have fewer meetings; on the contrary they have more, due to the necessity of pre-practice planning meetings which occur daily. One of the big differences you would see if you sat in on a college or professional sports team meeting is that they are often far more efficient than the typical department-wide forum. While both meetings *may* have an agenda, in my twenty years of coaching, I rarely saw one during the department meetings. We usually had no idea what was going to be covered in the meeting, thus could not prepare questions, talking points, or potential solutions for problems ahead of time. The athletic director would welcome everyone, give an overview of how some teams were doing (information also available on the website), invite a guest from some obscure department on campus to inform the coaches about something (that could have been covered in an email). From there the compliance (rules) director might play a quick game of "Compliance Jeopardy" covering rules (that 95% of us were already well aware of). The excitement would just be beginning as someone from the athletic training staff comes up to cover training room hours (also posted on the training room door) or review concussion policies (coaches had already taken a class on this). On one occasion the Chief of Police tried to explain the Run, Hide, or Fight model of dealing with a campus intruder. While of course this is a very serious subject, his brief explanation was difficult to follow and provided no action steps as to what specifically our student-athletes should know and what each team should do based on their location on campus. Here was another dreaded department-wide staff meeting concluded with little to no valuable takeaways and no clarity on why exactly we had the meeting. This happens thousands of times a week all over the country from small businesses to Fortune 100 companies.

When I first started in athletics, the meetings were met with much more enthusiasm by the staff, even though the topics and format were the same. The difference was—breakfast! The meetings had an assortment of palatable fare on a hot bar. That is, until someone decided it was an unnecessary expense. Breakfast was replaced by your choice of bagels or bagels, both of which tasted like they had been stored in garbage bags in the secretary's car since the last meeting. A friend of mine starts his meetings by pumping upbeat music into the room. Providing a small meal in conjunction with a staff meeting can add to the enthusiasm and engagement. You want to establish an interest and energy level and avoid having your crew cringe when they are notified of an upcoming meeting.

Coaches will regularly go into *their* staff or team meetings knowing exactly what will be covered and will come out of it with a plan and action steps. They are, in a word, efficient. Coaches often do a great job of knowing when it should be a full team meeting and when it should be just parts of the team. Let's look at a college football squad as an example. An NCAA FBS team can have up to eighty-five scholarship players plus an additional forty non-scholarship student-athletes should they choose to do so. There are times when an entire team meeting is necessary and other times when it is more effective to meet with smaller groups. If you walked into the football facility at any major university you would see designated breakout rooms with placards on the door identifying meeting areas for sub-groups within the team. For example, the offensive line would have their own room, special teams would have one, and the linebackers would occupy another.

During these position specific meetings, many teams break it down even further by having the players sit in the same spots they would occupy on the field. If we use the offensive line as an illustration, sitting in a row from left to right would be the left tackle, the left guard, the center, the right guard, and the right tackle. The reserve players for each of these positions would be sitting in their own row in the same order. This serves several purposes during the meeting or film session. Remember back to our chapter on culture and getting ahead of conflict by building relationships? One of the concepts was to pair players together who occupy space on the field in proximity to each other in order to build relationships because they will need to have great communication during competition. This seating configuration adds the same value. Over the course of a season, teammates are usually in meetings several times a week and these players become a more closely gelled unit. Another reason this arrangement is used is because it allows the group to visually relate to the exact scenario unfolding on the coach's whiteboard or video screen. How they are lined up in the row is identical to how they were lined up for the play—now projecting in front of them. Micro-conversations can occur quickly between the left tackle and the left guard if a play on the screen went awry that involved them specifically. Problem solving becomes more efficient.

I'm not suggesting that corporate America needs to have assigned seating, although there certainly could be some benefits. Yet there are some unique opportunities presented that, with some creativity, could turn the monthly meeting into something more valuable than it is currently. In addition to relationship building among similar positions as illustrated above, there is also the potential for interdepartmental team building which could help with cross-collaboration. In one particular athletic department all-staff meeting, we were instructed to find another person with whom we did not have regular interaction and learn a few things about them. The purpose of this wasn't really to learn a new fact about a co-worker; it was to build a connection outside of our own staff. I was a head coach and paired up with an assistant coach from another team with whom I had never had a prior conversation. Three months later this staff member had helped us to completely overhaul our on-campus recruiting visits due to some great pointers on how her program organized visits and tours for their top recruits. Cross-departmental collaboration at work.

Another benefit is participation and engagement. In small group, or breakout meetings, players and employees alike are more willing to be involved in the conversation than they would as part of a large group. Ask a question at your next meeting with one-hundred people in the room and you will probably have 5% to 10% who raise their hands to answer. Ask the same question to a group of ten and you will most likely get 50% or higher who have their hands in the air. The most obvious benefit of these sub-group meetings is that it does not waste the time of other people who do not need this information.

Staying with the football meeting scenario, I read an interesting story about the former University of Oregon football coach, Chip Kelly. While at UO, Coach Kelly brought in a paid consultant to sit in team and position meetings in order to assess the quality and efficiency of these meetings. This was a top program, competing for national championships, and yet the attention given to how meetings were run was important enough for Kelly to hire a consultant. In terms of employee engagement, most companies seriously underestimate the opportunity and the significance that well-timed, well-run, and well-organized meetings can have. One of the best and most concise business meeting formats I have seen comes from a chapter in the book *Traction* by Gino Wickman. Consider using it as a template for your own meetings.

BLUEPRINT FOR ACTION

You are now armed with potent strategies to forever improve engagement levels, reform your culture, and take control over your corporate destiny.

The first thing to do is to anonymously survey a population (or all) of your company with the goal of determining a baseline of corporate components that affect engagement. You can pay for this process or use the survey I develop and lay out in the final chapter. My model will allow you to identify specific engagement deficiencies and then use the corresponding book chapter to target improvement. Using my survey you will garner information with which to identify general engagement issues companywide. Should you desire to break this down to a more granular level, you can add more information to the questionnaire such as which department each employee completing the survey works in. This will help determine specific department (or manager) strengths and weaknesses.

Start by using the results to target the two areas that appear to be the most deficient. The results in one area may be alarming enough for you to probe further with more detailed questions. The clearer the information you have, the more efficient you can be solving the problem. If, for example, it is apparent that many employees simply don't feel valued, the 'Matter' chapter of the book would be a good place to begin training senior staff and managers. Simply bringing awareness to the engagement shortcoming is a good start but it must be followed with the question of "Why do employees not feel valued?" If you have a version of a leadership council (not just senior level managers) they may very well be able to answer the "why."

Because of the significance of workplace culture, you may want to incorporate several questions around it. Take the previous breakdown of the word CULTURE and incorporate a question which will provide you with information about: how creativity is valued, if there is a united vision, if individual accountability (liability) is clear and so on, until you cover all seven pillars of culture.

Hopefully you were able to identify an area that does not appear to be a shortcoming and is, rather, a strength. While addressing the two deficient areas, be sure to continue to build on the strength.

If you know your engagement levels are poor, you do not technically need a survey, but you will then lose out on creating a baseline with which to measure the improvement that will come with the implementation of $E=MC^4$ and the subsequent chapters.

Here are some final thoughts for organizing your roll out plan to boost engagement and transform culture:

1. Bring me in for a Train the Trainer program with management and leaders.

2. Require all managers to read *Engage, Excel, Exceed* and incorporate one chapter to review at the start of each weekly meeting.

3. Involve Human Resources in the process. HR can be a tremendous resource for implementing an engagement program.

4. Create a leadership council and empower them to construct an implementation plan using *Engage, Excel, Exceed.*

ENGAGEMENT QUESTIONS

In order to assess where your business falls on the engagement scale, consider administering an anonymous survey to your employees. You can create your own questions or use these as a template. If you are aware that your work place has no vision or definable culture, don't avoid the survey due to the fear of low score.

1. How VALUED do you feel by your company?

☐ Extremely valued

☐ Very valued

☐ Somewhat valued

☐ Not so valued

☐ Not at all valued

2. How effectively does your manager COMMUNICATE with you?

☐ Extremely effectively

☐ Very effectively

☐ Somewhat effectively

☐ Not so effectively

☐ Not at all effectively

3. How CONNECTED do you feel to your manager?

☐ Extremely connected

☐ Very connected

☐ Somewhat connected

☐ Not so connected

☐ Not at all connected

4. How effectively are you MANAGED/ COACHED by your manager?

☐ Extremely effectively

☐ Very effectively

☐ Somewhat effectively

☐ Not so effectively

☐ Not at all effectively

5. How clearly could you explain your organization's VISION?

☐ Extremely clearly

☐ Very clearly

☐ Somewhat clearly

☐ Not so clearly

☐ Not at all clearly

6. How clearly could you explain your organization's CULTURE?

☐ Extremely clearly

☐ Very clearly

☐ Somewhat clearly

☐ Not so clearly

☐ Not at all clearly

7. How effective is your annual or mid-year REVIEW?

☐ Extremely effective

☐ Very effective

☐ Somewhat effective

☐ Not so effective

☐ Not at all effective

☐ Not applicable to me

8. How effective is the GOAL SETTING process at your organization?

☐ Extremely effective

☐ Very effective

☐ Somewhat effective

☐ Not so effective

☐ Not at all effective

☐ Not applicable to me

9. How effective and efficient are your organization's MEETINGS?

☐ Extremely

☐ Very

☐ Somewhat

☐ Not so much

☐ Not at all

ABOUT WOODY SHERWOOD

Woody Sherwood grew up just outside of Washington D.C. in Rockville, Maryland. He graduated from Xavier University in Cincinnati, where he earned a Bachelor of Science in Psychology while playing NCAA D1 soccer. Sherwood also received his Master's Degree in Education from Xavier. He spent over two decades coaching college soccer. His stops include Towson University, Butler University, The University of Louisville, Indiana University, and Xavier University. After leaving coaching, he took his coaching and leadership skillset to corporate America, joining Rockwell Laser Industries in 2016. Additionally, he is an Instrument Rated Private Pilot, along with having his complex, high-performance and tailwheel endorsements.

Sherwood is a professional speaker and can be booked for corporate and civic events. Woody can be reached through his website, www.woodyspeaks.com or at info@woodyspeaks.com.

Made in the USA
Monee, IL
16 June 2020